MW00975323

PZ'S PANOPTICON

An Off-The-Wall Guide

To World Religion

By Paul F. M. Zahl

Mockingbird Ministries, Inc

Charlottesville, VA

Copyright © 2013 by Mockingbird Ministries

Mockingbird Ministries

100 West Jefferson Street

Charlottesville, VA 22902

www.mbird.com

All rights reserved.

No part of this book may be used or reproduced in any manner whatsoever without written permission, except in the case of brief quotations embodied in critical articles or reviews.

Cover design by Stephanie Fishwick. Edited by William McDavid. Published 2013 and printed by Createspace.com in the United States of America.

ISBN-13: 978-1492989240

ISBN-10: 149298924X

Disclaimer:

MOCKINGBIRD MINISTRIES ("MOCKINGBIRD") IS AN INDEPENDENT NOT-FOR-PROFIT MINISTRY SEEKING TO CONNECT, COMMENT UPON AND EXPLORE THE CHRISTIAN FAITH WITH AND THROUGH CONTEMPORARY CULTURE. MOCKINGBIRD FULLY DISCLAIMS ANY SPONSORSHIP, ASSOCIATION OR CONNECTION WITH ANY OF THE AUTHORS, ARTISTS OR PUBLICATIONS QUOTED OR REFERENCED HEREIN. THE CONTENT IS INTENDED FOR THE PURPOSE OF COMMENTARY, STUDY, DISCUSSION, AND LITERARY OR RELIGIOUS CRITIQUE. LIKEWISE, MOCKINGBIRD DISCLAIMS ANY AFFILIATION, SPONSORSHIP OR CONNECTION WITH ANY OTHER ENTITY USING THE WORDS "MOCKINGBIRD" AND "MINISTRIES" ALONE OR IN COMBINATION.

PZ'S PANOPTICON

Contents

Introduction

This book is a short guide to world religion. It is written from a subjective and personal standpoint. It is called *PZ's Panopticon*, as explained in chapter one; and consists of views of organized world religions, such as Christianity and Hinduism, as well as religions that are not called religions, such as celebrity and power. It is the result of a lifetime's study of religion.

From early exposure to Christian Science and Episcopalianism; to prep-school classes in 'Sacred Studies' under the legendary John Claiborne Davis at St. Alban's School in Washington, D.C.; and on to my first undergraduate study of religion at the University of North Carolina-Chapel Hill.

At Chapel Hill my teachers included John Howard Schutz (New Testament), Samuel S. Hill (American religious history), and William J. Peck (comparative religion).

At Harvard College, to which I transferred in 1970, I was the first undergraduate concentrator in the Department of Special Studies. My *A.B.* degree was awarded in "Hellenism and Christian Origins". At Harvard I studied under Zeph

Stewart (classics) and George Williams (church history).

At the University of Nottingham, James Dunn supervised my *M.Phil.*, which concerned the atonement of Christ in the Synoptic Gospels as it related to Christ's self-under-standing.

At Tübingen, beginning with the spring semester of 1992 through the fall semester of 1994, I was Jürgen Moltmann's last overseas doctoral student. I was also *wissenschaftliche Hilfskraft*, i.e., scientific assistant, to Peter Stuhlmacher.

Finally, I was privileged to write my Tübingen doctoral dissertation on the theology of Ernst Käsemann, who was present during that entire period. This dissertation was published by Calwer Verlag Stuttgart in 1996 under its original title, *Die Rechtfertigungslehre Ernst Käsemanns.* Herr Käsemann died in 1998.

I offer these *bona fides* to illustrate the interests and per-sonal history that lie behind *An Off-the-Wall Guide to World Religion.* Almost the most important element in the search for truth is one's teachers. They may even be the most im-portant element.

My book is therefore dedicated to Thomas W. Calhoun, Ph.D.

I would like to thank Dr. Simeon Zahl, of St. John's Col-lege, Oxford, for his constructive comments during the final phase of writing; and Will McDavid, of Mockingbird, for his artful and intelligent work as editor.

PZ's Panopticon

A panopticon is a building that is designed in order that you can see, from one stationery position within the building, every space or room of the interior. It is often in the shape of a semi-circle.

Some of the first panopticons were designs for prisons. The prison guard could sit in a central station and see into every cell, thus keeping watch over all the prisoners.

The 20th-century French philosopher Michel Foucault was interested in panopticon prisons because he believed they augured the future of centralized surveillance in cultures of control. I think Foucault was right about that.

In Protestant countries during the 18th and early 19th centuries, churches were often constructed in the shape of half circles, so that the minister, speaking from a high pulpit, could see every member of the congregation; and they, him.

Access, not control

Unlike panopticon prisons, however, the point of panopticon churches was access. They were designed like theaters, so that the inspired speaker at the center could both be seen and heard by everyone. Christopher Wren called such places of worship "auditory churches". In Hamburg there is an extreme example of such a Protestant church. It is called the "Michaeliskirche" – St. Michael's Church. When you go inside, you think you are in an opera house. By placing the minister at the center point of the design, the congregation have direct eye-contact with what they came for, a good sermon; and the preacher has direct eye-contact with them.

This short guide to world religion is a panopticon.

I, as the author, am in the central position, and am observing the religions of the world from that point. This makes it a subjective and personal book, a book of impressions based on life experience. It is not about controlling what I see, but is about seeing things for myself. What does religion mean to me? And not just "me", but dying me! For PZ's panopticon is actually a near-death experience.

Nos morituri

After 32 years of professional service in the field of religion, I had a sudden near-death experience. It happened at a specific time in a specific place. Everything I think about religion now comes through the panopticon of that near-death experience.

Much of what I had thought about religion prior to my near-death experience changed during it, within a time period of approximately ten minutes. Much of what I had thought about myself changed, too, and again, in approximately ten minutes.

This guide to world religion is written from a position of post-traumatic stress.

Ten minutes to lift-off

The result of a single period of ten minutes was a changed understanding of my own religion, which is Christianity. This turned into a changed understanding of other religions, too, such as Hinduism and Buddhism. But it was really a changed understanding of myself. A changed understanding of myself caused the "panopticon" of my life to move. The observer changed, therefore his location changed. His "angle" on everything changed.

PZ's Panopticon is a distillation of what I now, at the age of 62, see; or think I see. It represents a reconstruction of Christianity as I now practice it and think it, and the reconstruction of a lifetime's reflection on religious subjects. In some ways I have more faith now than I ever had before. In other ways I can't paddle fast enough away from certain associations and ideologies that were important to me once. I'm paddling a little slower now than I did at first.

There is a down side to this change. Sometimes I reach for a railing or buoy or a lifeboat, and don't have one. Like the man in Thomas Cole's "Hudson River" cycle of paintings "The Journey of Life", which was painted in 1842, I don't know where I am heading a lot of the time. Yet I haven't lost faith, the hope really, that my "bark" will end its journey in the kind of serene and quiet lake envisioned at the end of Cole's cycle of paintings. I am just not there yet.

What do I see now? What are the "varieties of religious experience" (William James) that exist around me? What do world religions look like at the end of a lifetime of religious study and religious practice? In the sphere of death and life, of permanence and change, "What is truth?" (John 18:38).

The Panopticon is You

Someone said to me, "The purpose of life is to find out who you are, and who God is." Thatv sounded right. It echoed the "order" of wisdom in my own religion, and in most world religions. That is, you have to stand in a proper relationship to yourself before you can understand the world around you, let alone God.

You can't understand what is going on around you from a position of superiority or looking down. You are carrying too much baggage, most of it inside you, for you to be able to do that. Moreover, a clamoring part of you is trying to control, or manage, the data you are getting from the world. How can you manage something that you can barely see as it really is, in its True Colors (Cyndi Lauper)?

A big emphasis of Eastern religion is on "clearing the air" inside you, clearing your mind from the constant static arising from your inner monologue, so that you can see what's in front of you. If you don't clear your mind – if you don't use a 'Mac Cleaner' – then you are receiving your impressions of reality through mental filters. These filters get in the way of seeing things as they are.

When the Christian religion talks about "repentance" or "contrition", it is talking about what another, Eastern religion calls "right views" of yourself. You are not the master of your fate, and no amount of saying you are is going to change the fact that you are not. You are a contingent person. This means that you are subject to circumstances beyond your control. An accurate view of life means accepting this.

Not long ago an acquaintance of mine served a two-month prison sentence. He was almost 90 years old when he entered the prison. He had to go everywhere he went in a wheelchair.

When my wife and I first knew him, our acquaintance was rich and famous. Whenever he came to a party, he was the instant guest of honor. That was mainly because of his name, his presumed wealth, and his family connections.

Now this man has served a prison sentence. In photographs that we see online, he and his wife, who did not go to prison, look like wrecks of themselves. How else can you see life, in the face of such a fall, other than as a condition of enforced humility before the blows of experience?

My point is that repentance and contrition are traditional religious words for an evergreen truth: "We brought nothing into this world, and it is certain we can carry nothing out" (1 Timothy 6:7, KJV).

"Who are you?" (The Who)

The best panopticon to see with is your dying

A panopticon is the view-finder through which you look at what is all around you. It is how you see what is there, and it is your outlook on the world.

The best panopticon to see with is the panopticon of your dying.

15

It is received wisdom that just before a person dies, they see their whole life passing in front of them. People who fell to their death (but were somehow saved), or who were about to be executed (but were spared at the last minute), or who were staring straight ahead as their car crashed into a tree (but survived the crash): these people often report that just before "impact", their entire life passed before their eyes.

A more contemporary form of those reports comes when a person has died on the operating table but is revived and brought "back". The person reports what they saw. Many who have come back in this way say that they felt themselves floating in the air, over themselves. They felt as if they were looking down on themselves. They were looking down as if from the ceiling, watching as the doctors tried to revive their body. They were detached, in other words, at the point of death, from their physical self; and seemed to exist for a while outside it.

There will probably always be controversy about "near-death" experiences, and there are several theories about them. But I don't think anyone would disagree with the idea that *something* of a dis-attaching occurs at death. You can just call it a dis-attaching of consciousness. Whoever or whatever was in your body – let's say, "life" – is, following death, no longer present. All you need to do is observe a dead body for a little while, or touch it, to realize that something has gone out of it. This is the experience people have in funeral homes. They go up to the front and look at the body of the deceased, and they become *certain* that the person they knew is no longer there.

There is something about the preface to death's "detaching" from the body, which is this lightning perception of your whole life passing in front of you from birth to now, that is a good panopticon. You see everything you ever did and everything that ever happened to you. You may not be able to interpret what you see, but you see a lot.

Cold Lazarus

Dennis Potter, the English writer for television, described an experience like this in a somewhat autobiographical science-fiction script for the BBC entitled *Cold Lazarus*. At least twice in *Cold Lazarus*, Potter portrayed a character whose whole life whizzes before his eyes, mentally, like a speeded-up movie.

Dennis Potter wrote *Cold Lazarus* in the last weeks before he died. He knew he was dying and wanted to record his dying process. (His body was shutting down, and he kept himself alive by means of daily "cocktails" of medicine which prolonged his life so he could finish *Cold Lazarus*. Potter's subjective impressions of all this were recorded on April 5, 1994 in a television interview conducted by Melvyn Bragg.)

The best panopticon, which means the truest outlook on your life as a whole, is the approach of death.

"This can't be happening."

It happened to me.

It didn't happen to me the way it happened to Dennis Potter. I am still in my body and still in good health. But something happened that shut me down, or rather, called me into total question as a person. My old self, or "old man", to quote St. Paul, was put to death, and it happened fast.

In 2007 I held a fairly high management position in my profession, and had recently come from another management position that was quite prestigious, at least in the city where I had held the job. I had written several books and was a speaker in some demand within my professional circle. I also had a wonderful wife, and still do; and three much loved and thriving adult children.

On a Friday morning in January 2007, I was given a document to read which showed me that I had been living in an environment of which I really knew nothing. I was theoretically the "head", or C.E.O., of that environment, which was an extension of the professional environment in which I had worked for over 30 years; but the words I was reading revealed that I had been completely unaware of what was going on. As I read the words in front of me, I began to ask myself, "Can it be true that this document exists? Can this really be happening?"

"Sweet dreams and flying machines"

Right after saying that to myself, another thought came to me:

"If what I am reading is real, then everything up to now in my life, or almost everything, has been *un*-real. What I thought was true may not now be so – that is, if *this* is true."

The three or four pages I was reading were like a tablecloth you can pull out from under a set table, spilling all the dishes and silver and crystal on the ground. One yank and everything breaks. "Sweet dreams and flying machines in pieces on the ground." (James Taylor)

Within about ten minutes, I can honestly say that my old self was murdered.

"Here lies Paul F. M. Zahl. He seems to have been wrong about everything."

The document in front of him told him he had been living in the country of the blind. It screamed, the existence of the document screamed: you were wrong about your friends, you were wrong about your work, you are wrong about the present, you were wrong about the past, you were wrong about your future. You've been on the wrong side, for crying out loud!

Most of all, and this was completely devastating: you were wrong about yourself.

To put it in terms of this book: as a living panopticon, as an observer of my world, let alone the chief actor in it, I had been looking out on the world with the wrong pair of eyes.

Later it turned out that 'Paul Zahl' had not been wrong about everything. Some things he had believed prior to his murder proved, on reflection, to have been right. But he himself – the man! – had been on the wrong track.

Before you start saying, "Nothing like that has ever happened to *me*. I have had my moments, and certainly some moments of self-doubt and thoughts of futility, but nothing quite like what you are saying" – before you start saying that to yourself, think again.

Why do people kill themselves?

Why do people kill themselves? Not you, the reader of this book, obviously. You are reading it! But think how many people take their own lives. It is a taboo subject, in general; and I have been in the pastorate for 38 years. But a great many people, of most of whom I would never have thought to expect it, let alone the families and friends they left behind, have taken their own lives. You could almost say that suicide is an epidemic in the world we live in. The statistics say that suicide is now an epidemic.

People commit suicide for as many reasons as there are people. But in almost all cases of sudden suicide, there is a breaking point, what is today called a "tipping point". Then BANG!: They're dead.

I have buried too many suicides, lovely people whom I loved and whose act took everyone by surprise. I mean, everyone, though people will sometimes say, "I wasn't a bit surprised when I heard" (to which my unspoken reply is, "Then why didn't you reach out to her?"). But something triggered the act. It didn't just "happen".

The point is, many people have experienced personal tipping points in their lives. Maybe you have. Many can remember a moment in time when everything they were doing felt false, when everyone they knew seemed to count for nothing, and when love felt like a dream and hell was the ground you were standing on.

In my own case, thoughts of suicide did not occur to me on that January Friday in 2007. But I also knew, and knew for certain – and still feel this way – that my old life was over. It was completely over, and I had been murdered.

Would Julius Caesar have felt this way if he had recovered from the wounds he received on the Ides of March? Would Caesar have wanted to stay in Rome and serve out his term as Consul? Or would he have fled pell-mell to the desert and asked for only one human comfort: Cleopatra.

I know what I would have done. And I did it.

I fled to the desert.

This book is the result of four years in the desert.

Three characteristics of a near-death panopticon

This guide to world religion is written through the lens of a near-death panopticon. It takes the position of a person who finds himself floating up the wall, on the ceiling, looking down helplessly as the surgeons try to save his body on the operating table.

People are trying to save his life. Part of him wants to go back to his life. Another part of him is glad to be out of it, relieved to be out of the fight. Whatever happens, the near-dead has not quite gone on yet. He can't help but be interested in the outcome.

Here are three characteristics of a near-death panopticon:

First, a near-death panopticon is partly detached from what it sees. It is not *completely* detached, for "I ain't dead yet". But a near-death panopticon is not seeing at the same level from which I used to see. The viewer is one stage removed.

Alfred Hitchcock often used an overhead camera angle that he called "the God's-eye view". He used this angle many times, from *The Paradine Case* (1947) to *North by Northwest* (1959) to *The Birds* (1963) to his last movie, *Family Plot* (1976). Hitchcock got you to look down on the action and gain considerable perspective on it. He made you see more than you had seen earlier, when the camera was at ground-floor level.

A near-death panopticon is semi-detached.

Second, a near-death panopticon observes two different forms of the self, two different subjectivities. It sees them both at the same time.

The first subjectivity is the person at ground-level whom the doctors are trying to revive. That person is 'Paul F. M. Zahl', or 'P.T. Barnum', or 'Richard Matheson', each of whom, like everybody else at the point of death, is struggling to hold on to the fragile body-mind connection that was given this or that name at birth and who lives as if he or she is the sole proprietor of such a person.

But there is a second self. This is the self who is probably closer to the person on the ceiling. The second self is different in essence and quality, maybe bigger, than the person struggling to survive on the surface below. He or she, the bigger person, survives (somehow) after the physical dis-connection from the self underneath that is in furious motion to keep hold on physical life.

Or, if you don't want to use the language of survival – because you don't believe in survival – maybe it's enough just to differentiate the latter from the former. Whatever the chances of continuance may or may not be for some part of you, you do know that the person below who is struggling, and the person above who is floating, are different. The fact that one can observe the other means that they are different.

When we say to someone we love who is dying, "Let go, dear Paul. It is time for you to let go", we are talking about two subjectivities: the fighting being that is 'Paul Zahl' and the being who is watching the fight.

Unfortunately, the furious fight on the earth below cannot be won. It is impossible for the first subject to hold on, "world without end". Resisting physical death is a day at the Alamo, a weekend in Stalingrad.

Whatever words we want to give it, there is a dual identity to human selves that the coming of death makes apparent. The panopticon I am talking about is characterized by a felt transcendence on the part of the second self. The religions of the world are best seen, their intentions and practices best observed, from a place as near as possible to transcendence. A survey of world religion, and probably a guide to almost anything, requires Alfred Hitchcock's God's-Eye view.

THIRD, a near-death panopticon contains the possibility of religious wisdom. Poised on the frontier between tran-scendence and personal extinction, it has an interest in the questions that religion asks. This is not a mental or concep-tual "stake", for it is no longer a question of ideas battling it out to win a prize. Ideas as such don't save the person who is fighting for his life on the operating table, or even in his bed at home. (Many people die suddenly in their bed at home. How many times have I been called to be present with someone who died in their sleep and was just discovered by... the super!)

Religion is not about the superiority of one concept in comparison to another concept.

Rather, religion is about *salvation* in the most imminent sense of the word. Religion is about saving your life, saving who you are from the defeat and extinction that death brings to your first subjectivity; and rescuing you, or some essence and aspect of you, in favor of some sort of continuity with who you were before you were born. Ideological secularism is a form of religion, too, by the way, because it is a thought-process about reality with a view to an absolutely solo dogged life that is exclusive to the exact period between your birth and your death.

IHOP

Who is the real you?

Are you the person being looked down upon from the ceiling, the person struggling to be revived in the middle of a hospital "Code Red"?

Or are you the person doing the looking down, someone who is both you and not you?

We know from funerals, and wakes and viewings that the person on the operating table or in intensive care ends. At the funeral, that person is not present. Lesson One of funeral parlors is that the person you see in the casket is not your mother, or your father, or your husband, or your child.

It is "sure and certain" (*Book of Common Prayer*) that the person who was alive and whom you (hopefully) loved, at least a little, is not the same as the body in the casket, with its pancake makeup and dirty eyeglasses placed over the pancaked nose at the wrong angle and Sunday suit you haven't seen for years that's probably been split down the back but you can't see, that is "on view".

Required question

The question raised by the problem of our connection with the body, or rather, our empirically severed-at-death connection with the body we used to live in, is a question that demands to be asked, and even if it cannot be answered. The question demands to be asked. Religions ask the question. They should get some credit.

If you don't ask the question – no matter whether you can answer it or not, that's not the point; you still have to ask it – you are refusing to look at the most puzzling and most defeating phenomenon of life, which is the end of life. In my opinion, human beings are required to "make inquiries" (Scotland Yard) concerning the meaning of life's end. You don't have to be "religious" in a formal sense to have to do that. But you are required to ask the question. It's part of *The Rules of the Game* (Jean Renoir).

All this is why a near-death panopticon requires that humans examine religion. By religion, I mean religion in a wide meaning. A near-death panopticon is a kind of telescope that tilts to the side of getting a view of past religious wisdom in hope of getting some understanding that could help the floater-self before he or she drifts away and loses all substantiation. The floater needs help this minute.

That is the reason I became instantly interested in world religion, not just my own inherited form of it, in the immediate aftermath of the nuclear flash that lit up all my canyons on a January Friday in 2007. I became an instantaneous candidate for any and all options that might possibly convey some comfort and aid. No possible point of view was off the table. For "I could not foresee/This thing happening to me." (Rolling Stones)

The cartoonist Drew Friedman drew a picture entitled "Sitcom Characters in Search of Enlightenment". In it you can see 'Lucy' of *I Love Lucy* and 'Gomer Pyle' from *The Andy Griffith Show* and 'Maynard G. Krebs' from *The Many Loves of Dobie Gillis*, and a multitude of familiar faces from old TV comedy shows. These characters are sitting in the reading room of a public library, thumbing through the classics of world wisdom, from Dickens to Freud to Dostoyevsky. It's a funny and original idea, and is perfectly illustrated by the artist. It portrays, from left field, the almost universal search, in light of death, for a panopticon of world religion.

Pecking our way out

Gerald Heard, who was a friend and mentor to the novelists Aldous Huxley and Christopher Isherwood, said that human beings are like baby chicks trying to get themselves hatched. We are all in the position of needing to free ourselves from an encircling shell. We poke our little beaks against the shell, trying for the life of us to break out into the open air. Everyone is pecking and pecking away, with greater or lesser degrees of success. Some get out, many get out; but some are unable to penetrate the shell. These last chicks cannot escape, and finally give up and die. Time is not on their side.

This is a faithful picture of the human struggle, at least as I see it. We are trapped inside a hardened membrane, and have got to get out. We put our whole self into the struggle to get out. It is where religion enters, and not just formal religion. People are having to work so hard to find their way through that they will try anything, or anyone, that can help. "I get by with a little help from my friends" (Lennon/Mc-Cartney). Such friends, whoever or whatever they are, have a saving role, though they can also be chimaeras. "Whatever gets you through the night, it's all right" (John Lennon).

Religions that are not called religions

A near-death panopticon will not limit itself to traditional or formal religions, such as Hinduism or Christianity. A near-death panopticon is crying, "Help!" If it takes acquisition to make me feel better, well, that may be a kind of religion for me. If it takes a sexual connection to make me feel better, well, again, that may be a kind of religion. If it takes fame and celebrity to do it, then again, it may be a kind of religion. And so on, through family as my religion, my children as my religion, ideology (left, right, and center) as my religion, and power as my religion. The world's organized religions are not so different, in hoped-for impact, as these "everyday" listed helps. All of them, from fame to children, from sex to Buddhism, from a-theism to Hinduism, from wealth to Islam: "Whatever gets you through the night, it's all right."

Waltari and the 'Beats'

Mika Waltari was a Finnish writer who specialized in panopticons of near- death. In each of his historical novels, one of which, *The Egyptian*, became an international bestseller in 1949, Waltari would introduce a young man in search of himself and, therefore, of truth; and often, too, of God. The hero would mature, but through suffering.

By the conclusion of almost all of Waltari's novels, the hero of the book would have become a "panopticon" of seared-away flesh and superfluities – just like our man on the ceiling, looking back on his life from a reflective position of dis-attachment brought about through exile or last-minute pardon, and with the wisdom that comes from withered-ness, that is, the complete deflation of his acquisitive, aggrandizing self. The panopticon of near-death would have brought Waltari's characteristic hero to something like the beaten-down position of Jack Kerouac and the Beat Poets[1]:

> *"Pull my daisy*
> *Tip my cup*
> *All my doors are open*
> *Cut my thoughts for coconuts*
> *All my eggs are broken"*

Dark Angel

In a typically perceptive passage, Waltari puts the following words into the mouth of his hero, as 'Johannes Angelos' tells his life's story to the woman he loves. The passage occurs in *The Dark Angel* (1953)[2]:

> "Why do you suppose I have told you so much about myself? To pass the time, perhaps, or to make myself interesting in your eyes?... No. I wanted to show you that nothing means what you think it means, or what you have been brought up to believe. Riches and poverty, power and fear, honor and shame, wisdom and stupidity, ugliness and beauty, good and evil – nothing

---

1 "Pull My Daisy", Lyrics by Jack Kerouac and Allen Ginsberg, from *Pull My Daisy. Text by Jack Kerouac for the film by Robert Frank and Alfred Leslie* (Goettingen: Steidl, 2008; First Grove Press Edition 1961), 1.

2 Mika Waltari, *The Dark Angel*. Translated by Naomi Walford (New York: G.P. Putnam's Sons, 1953), 104.

has any significance in itself. The only thing that has significance is what we make of ourselves and what we desire to be... I have stripped myself of everything. I am nothing. And for me this is the highest that mortals can attain..."

That is a panopticon of near-death, which is another way of saying, the panopticon of death as experienced within the world of physical life. It is the wisdom of the Ancient of Days because it is the wisdom of the inward.

Religion, which is a way of saying the spiritual element of life, is the exploration of human inwardness. It observes the outward, but through the lens of the inward. Because the outward seems so real, even though the outward is actually always in flux, the religious question – "Help me!" – often fixes itself on outward objects. For that reason it can be disappointed. The search for inward answers in terms of outward conditions or attainments is disappointed almost as often as it is rewarded.

A panopticon of near-death, which, whether we like it or not, is occasioned by the unsatisfactoriness of the objects of desire in the visible world – they don't deliver what they promise – is the vantage point from which the varying promises of the world religions, i.e., Vedanta, Christianity, Buddhism, Islam, etc.; and world religions lower case, i.e., sex, acquisition, family, fame, ideology, and power, can be compared and weighed. A panopticon of near-death, which is the death of the self, or at least one of the selves, prior to our physical death, is the benchmark for this comparative study of religion. It is ground zero of this book.

Auditioning for the lead role

One more step needs to be taken before this tour of world religion can begin. It is implicit in what has been said, but still needs to be "vetted":

Who exactly is the "self" floating on the ceiling, and how does that self relate to the other "self", the self who is struggling for life at ground level? *Who is the real lead in this play?* If there are actually two selves in the opening scene, which of the two is holding the panopticon? Whose are *The Eyes of Laura Mars* (1978)?

Most religions postulate a division or two-ness within the human being. St. Paul spoke of the Old or Natural Man and the New Man. Greek philosophy spoke of the Many and the One, by which persons are seeking, or rather, retrieving, Oneness within the ever-changing many-ness of their sense-perceptive lives. Buddhism speaks of the desiring self and the self that has extinguished all desire and is therefore no longer a self at all in the way that the desiring self thought it was. Even everyday human desires, for "family, art, causes, new shoes" (Joss Whedon), distinguish between the self that I am that has not, and the self that I could become if only I had.

Aldous Huxley portrayed the wisdom of mysticism, both East and West, as a "perennial philosophy", according to which the inward alone is real; and to find the true self, you have to go within. There is only One (Reality), of which my inward conscious self is a temporary or "loaned-out" part. But I can only find this out, and discover the One who exists beneath and within the many, when I begin to give up my involvement with my apparent self. I have to dis-attach from my apparent self in order to begin to find my real self.

In the metaphor of preparing to produce a play, who is the lead actor in this play? Who has the starring role? Who holds the panopticon of life?

"Baby Driver" (Paul Simon)

One thing I have found out for myself and "mine eyes shall behold, and not as a stranger" (*Book of Common Prayer*) is that religion is not about controlling, shaping, or even instructing the self that I used to think I am. It is not about 'Paul Zahl' trying to gain control over his circumstances, let alone trying to gain control over himself. That has never worked out, and 62 years of experience tell me it never will. "There's got to be a better way" (Frankie Goes to Hollywood). Whatever is true about my apparent self, which could be called my "ego", it is highly resistant, or better, obdurate. It doesn't like to be told what it should want or what it should do. It doesn't like to go along with anyone else's bright ideas.

Religions that are about subduing that particular driver – "They call me Baby Driver" – fail. Or at least they fail to do what they have set themselves up to do. No matter how noble they sound in maxim and aphorism, no matter how lofty their goals in terms of personal and social improvement, and high-mindedness, they don't work. Their problem is that they are trying to revive a patient, as we now see him, who is struggling against the inevitable, which is death, down in the operating theater. The "drowning pool" of failed efforts to re-animate the dead cannot be allowed to become the prime theater of life. If you think it is the scene of life's real action – and resolution – then it will turn into Vincent Price's *Theatre of Blood* (1973).

A religion that works needs to be a religion that is not having to work "over-time" to conquer the unconquerable. You could say that a religion which works has to have different raw material than the human "self" who is involved in a life-long action to deny and postpone the inevitable. Religion that works, in other words, is a question of "if you can't stand the heat, then get out of the kitchen." I am talking about religion as flight, not fight.

"A position which has become impossible"

At first hearing, this sounds like cowardice, the opposite of religion as good works, social improvement, and engaged optimism. But religion with those outstanding positive themes, when it is not anchored to the fact of death, and the near-death which permeates life, fails to deliver, by which I mean, "deliver us from evil" and help us face death. Practical religion takes the measure of the ego's impossible situation, and locates the solution to it outside the field of battle. As Gerald Heard put it, "The verb to escape is clear enough – it means to leave a position which has become impossible."[3]

The panopticon of life cannot be in the hands of the struggler down in ICU. He or she is losing the fight. There is no way under the sun by which the ego-life on that flat surface will be able to carry on forever, no matter what. It is too late for the extinguishing self to understand what is going on

3 Gerald Heard, "Is Mysticism Escapism?" in *Vedanta for the Western World*, Edited and with an Introduction by Christopher Isherwood (Hollywood: Vedanta Press, 1945), 29.

with it. All he and she can do is "keep on dancing (dancin' and a prancin', doing the jerk)" (The Gentrys, 1965), until they just collapse upon the ground.

The man on the ceiling is the one with the panopticon, not the man below. It is always too late for the man below. The raw material of him can't respond to treatment. It is the man on the ceiling to whom the religions of the world have got to have something to say. He is the man on the moon.

World Religions

Organized Religions of the West

The three great organized religions of the West are Judaism, Christianity, and Islam. Christianity was born from Judaism, then separated from it. Later, Islam was born partly as a reaction to Christian teaching concerning the Trinity.

Sometimes these three religions, which were inter-dependent in their origins but independent in their later development, are placed under the heading "religions of the book". The classification "religions of the book" refers to the reliance that Jews, Christians, and Muslims have on ancient sacred writings: The Law and the Prophets for Judaism; the New Testament for Christianity, although Christians give almost the same authority to the Law and the Prophets (i.e., the Old Testament) as they do to the New Testament; and the Qu'ran for Islam. There are other, later writings or written teachings that are regarded as canonical by many Jews, just as there are "apocryphal" books of the Old and the New Testaments that many Christians read in church. All of these sources, to greater or lesser degrees, are considered revelations from God.

Although it is true that the three great organized religions of the West have for many centuries been closely "monitored", or supervised, by authoritative books, they are not all that different in this respect from Hinduism and Buddhism in the East. Hinduism, too, has canonical Scriptures, these being the Vedas, the Upanishads, and the "Song of God", or Bhagavad-Gita; while Buddhism, or rather, schools of thought within Buddhism, have sutras of widely varying dates, and collections of the Buddha's teaching, some close to his lifetime and some quite far removed from his lifetime, that are studied with great reverence.

So yes, Judaism, Christianity, and Islam all have canonical scriptures for which believers and clergy would shed blood. And they have! Almost all religions of the world possess writings, artifacts, relics, or *something* that provides a sense of physical continuity with their earliest sacred origins.

A panopticon of near-death is not particularly focussed on written things.

Yes, our man on the ceiling is interested in aid and comfort. And yes, he will try to grab it wherever he can. Nevertheless, he is not interested in fine print.

To tell you the truth, in the situation he is in, he can barely read. He "hasn't got time for the pain" (Carly Simon).

Christianity

Christianity seems almost "tailor made" to be a help in time of need for people like our main character, near-dead and spelling out a message of invincible pain. But Christianity is often understood as the opposite of that. In fact, so different has Christianity become in presentation from what it really is in essence, that the contrast could almost make you believe in the existence of Satan. *What?*

A religious "fact on the ground" today is this:

To our near-dead victim of life, it is not likely that he has known Christianity to be anything other than the Grouch-Religion of the world. He has probably been so shaped by the invisible force-field of attitudes and assumptions that surrounds him, that he has barely been able to give a hearing to Christianity in its core form, which is a religion of mercy and forgiveness.

I said "Satan" above – and I mean by that, something malicious, a dog in the manger, a "horse with no name" (America) – because it becomes malice when a genuine possibility of help is actively prevented from getting to where it is needed. It is like blocking the road to a fire so that the fire-engines can't get through.

On the other hand, our man is near death. He has no here-and-now input except for the whoosh of his blood pressure and pain like an anvil on his chest. He is actually almost beyond the physical pain of his true situation. And he's got a fearful ringing in his ears. One thing is sure: he would probably take help from anywhere or anyone if he thought it would give him some surcease.

"Crying in the Chapel"

Let's imagine he were to get a message *back* from his SOS, faint as it sounded at first. It is the thread of a message with few words in it, just a phrase or two, to which he pricks up his ears.

Consider a person who says she has no religion, or almost no religion, but finds herself in church. Maybe it's a "funeral for a friend" (Elton John). The organist happens to play "Abide with Me" or the Navy Hymn. Suddenly the person is inexplicably – though it is not inexplicable – overcome by emotion. She starts sobbing. She starts shaking with sobbing. "How can this be happening?" she asks herself. She hates the feeling, but somehow also loves it, too.

People have experiences like this more than they let on. They don't necessarily want you to know they've had them, partly because it's embarrassing. It betrays some emotional hiddenness that is painful. Christianity, for it's often Christianity that's the "culprit", summons something up. It is through music or something like music, so it's a little inchoate, what St. Paul spoke of as "sighs too deep for words" (Romans 8:26). Christianity, partly because it's "in the air tonight" (Phil Collins) and people have been exposed to it, even if it was just your mother's prayer at your bedside when you were three, is the culprit.

I have heard this from hundreds of people over the years. Hundreds is not an exaggeration. "I'm not religious," they say. "But when I heard that 'song' at so-and-so's wedding or at my aunt's funeral in your church, I just dissolved. I don't understand it. I can't get over it. What happened?"

In a movie called *Good Luck Miss Wyckoff* (1979), which is based on a novel by William Inge, the main character is sitting in a high school auditorium listening to one of her students play a familiar piece on the piano by Mozart. The viewer of the movie knows already that 'Miss Wyckoff' is suffering acutely in her personal life. Suddenly, as she hears the beautiful notes of the familiar melody, she is overcome by emotion. She doesn't know why, but she is completely wiped out. She is also extremely embarrassed.

This kind of experience happens to people all the time in church.

Now let's put this inarticulate "something" in direct relation to our poor flailing floater, our dying 'Miss Wyckoff'. In that state, our hero is not only open to *anything*, but she can almost *only* hear the unspoken and unwritten. It will need to be very brief and very emotional. She is all feelings now. If she has any kind of hold at all on the panopticon, which by this point is probably not much more than a straw through which only faint light is coming, what can she see, or hear, from the ruined "City of God" that was once the religion of Christianity?

"Put an amen to it!"

That's a line from *The Searchers* (1956), when the John Wayne character is in a hurry to get away from a funeral so he can start tracking down the murderers of the people being buried. The urgency of the line expresses what people mean when they talk about "closure". There is something bad in the past that we are trying to get away from, and as soon as possible. We want closure so we can move forward unencumbered.

Our friend on the ceiling needs closure, on her life.

"Not Fade Away" (Rolling Stones)

Did you know that the origin of ghost stories is in the idea that the dead, or some of them, are still weighed down, almost literally, with things they have done in the past that won't let them "move on"? Something like weights is preventing them from moving on to wherever they are moving on to. The ghost in supernatural fiction has something on his mind. It "weighs" on him or her so heavily that the ghost is *held* by it, suspended between life and whatever is beyond or after life. And the living, *we*, inter-act most reluctantly with the ghost who still has the work to do. In classic literary ghost stories, such as Edith Wharton's "Afterward" or "The Beckoning Fair One" by Oliver Onions, the ghost gets "closure" by arranging for the evildoer from her or his life to be killed. Sometimes, though not as often, the ghost is benign, and helps an unrealized dream or hope of love to be realized, as in a mother's dying wish for her daughter to be married or a husband's dying regret in relation to his wife. When the past of the ghost is resolved, the "shade" of the ghost begins to fade away from involvement with its prior world. It is now at peace.

Our man on the cork ceiling is like a ghost. Or maybe not quite a ghost. But he thinks like a ghost. And the original, if faint, message of the world religion Christianity has something in it for him. It has something in it for ghosts everywhere, if only it can get through.

Erasure

The original message of Christianity is the message of the 100% forgiveness of sins. That is the faint though original message of closure on the past that the founder of Christianity sent.

The message of 100% forgiveness is explicit in almost every inter-action Christ ever had with people. He said that people need to be forgiven "seventy times seven" times (Matthew 18:22). He said that he "did not come into the world to condemn the world; but that the world might be saved through him" (John 3:17); and to the woman caught in adultery, "Neither do I condemn you" (John 8:11). He scored out the implications of his strange and seemingly unfair idea when he said, "Whoever has been forgiven little loves little" (Luke 7:47). Most memorably, he prayed to God to forgive the people who were killing him: "Father, forgive them, for they know not what they do" (Luke 23:34). Why try to prove that this was his message anyway? The hero of this book is not asking for proof. He is just asking for something that makes sense in his moment of crisis, and therefore comforts him. Try to see things from his point of view.

"Drawing a line through the past" – it is not only "closure", it's erasure – is exactly what a man or woman in near-death encounter desires to hear: "You can go now. That's all forgiven and forgotten. It's all right." By this is meant, your past is taken care of and doesn't have to be in front of you any more as you look ahead to what's next. All is forgiven. Begin the beguine.

People get nervous about this, or at least people who are not in the middle of near death. It sounds from the vantage point of the *other* self, the person on the operating table, or rather, the patient in pre-op, like a blessing on bad behavior. You say to yourself, "How can that bad person get off the hook just because God chooses to disregard the things he or she has done and says, 'Poof! All better now.' When it's all not better now." I don't know the answer to this question. It bothers me, too. But it doesn't bother me *much*, and I'll tell you why.

I'm still thinking about our "fool on the hill", the character on the ceiling. The fool is me. I know I am supposed to be concerned about the people I've hurt, and there are many, which I regret. I hope God can give them closure in the way they need. I really mean this. But right now *I* am the fool on the hill, and I don't know what to do. Obviously I can't go back and mend fences. It's too late, even though I'd like to. But given the desperate measures being taken below me, where med techs are "scrambling" – that's the word today for furious futility – to bring in more equipment to revive me, I am probably not going to be able to change things. Although it wasn't too late for Ebenezer Scrooge, though only by a hair – and I barely remember who Scrooge was, anyway – it is probably too late for me.

What I need to be is be forgiven.

"Death makes us all innocent."

A lyric passage about forgiveness in hindsight occurs in William Inge's last published novel, which was called *My Son is a Splendid Driver*. It was published in 1971. It is just one sentence, and reflects Inge's concept of serenity at the point of departure[4]:

"Death makes us all innocent, and weaves all our private

---

4 William Inge, *My Son is a Splendid Driver* (Boston and Toronto: Little Brown and Company, 1971), 220.

> hurts and griefs and wrongs into the fabric of time, and
> makes them part of eternity."

Inge wrote that sentence from the position of a precarious hold he had on the Christian insight concerning the relation of a peaceful death to the hope of innocence. He could barely say those words for himself, and took his own life two years after he wrote them. Yet it is the hope in the sentence that rings true. Our own panic-stricken hero is looking around himself in the most urgent and suffering search for a spark of hope. Near-death persons do this.

The mercy intrinsic to the teachings of Christ is something that is there from the beginning to the end. It is the crowning feature of what turned into the world's most populous religion.

I can't believe I ate the whole thing.

For quite a few people, there is something upsetting about the 100%-with-no-exceptions forgiveness that Jesus talked about. It is a feature that upsets conservatives. But it also upsets liberals. There is something in it to offend everybody. Except the person who needs it at the time.

What proves hard to swallow is the absolute character of it. Christ's forgiveness includes the worst offenders you can think of, but it also includes the pussycats of life – there aren't many pussycats, but there are a few – who have done nothing wrong or worthy of blame. It is a blanket forgiveness that puts a straight red line through the past. I write "red line" because the Old Story says that Christ's blood was shed in place of my blood. Dylan captured this on his 2012 album "Tempest": "I pay in blood/But not my own." It seems obvious that this is unfair. It seems to put *"The Good, the Bad and the Ugly"* (1966) all under the same protection. There is no distinction.

A familiar rationalization for Christ's universal forgiveness goes like this: "Well, yes, it *is* for everybody, but you have to ask for it. The offender can't receive it until he or she asks for it. Each person, good, bad, or a little bit of both, has to do his part. It won't do you any good if you don't first come forward and take it." That is a rationalization in service of explaining away the "full-service", 24/7 gas station that Christ's message actually is for all the cars on the road.

Can anyone really rationalize what Christ was saying when he said that people should be forgiven 490 times per action per person?

Yet that is exactly what the panopticon of life is seeing from its location in the hands of the person who is on the cork ceiling. Because there is no going back – it's probably almost definitely over, downstairs – the forgiveness Christ was talking about when he said things like that has to be this way. For a person who cannot go back, mercy is everything or nothing. 490 times to be forgiven per person per action is just about enough.

So yes, we can mute it or explain it and even limit it if our panopticon is sited in the human world at ground-level. At ground level, I'm a believer: in "zero tolerance" and "one strike you're out". But for the man between, who is really the man "Afterward" (Edith Wharton), it is too late for that. It is either now or never. No more strikes allowed.

Back story: Love's cause

In traditional Christian theology, Catholic, Protestant, and Eastern Orthodox, the finality of forgiveness is rooted in a single, unrepeatable, ancient action. This action is called the Atonement and was performed by Christ when he was crucified. It is the "back story" to a "front story", the front story being the rest, or peace, that a person has when his conscience, and really his whole life, is no longer plagued by accusation. It is the peace that comes from a quiet conscience.

If a quiet mind is the front story of Christian experience, the back story is the instrument or dynamic by which such a thing has become possible. A familiar way of putting this is: G.R.A.C.E., i.e., God's Redemption At Christ's Expense.

The truth that this kind of thinking expresses, by which a back story is required to explain a front story, is the fact of life that in life, nothing happens without a cause. God can't forgive sins "axiomatically" or by *fiat* because if He did so, He would be going against His justice. If God is in harmony, then His mercy and His justice cannot be in conflict. God is required by His nature as Harmony to be merciful and just, not merciful as opposed to just. On the other hand, God is required by His nature as Harmony to be just and merciful, not just as opposed to merciful. By definition God is the reconciliation of opposites, One (God) rather than a collection of Many. To quote Psalm 85, "Righteousness and peace have kissed each other" (v. 10).

Note, by the way, that we have abruptly entered a new world: religious abstraction! And I thought I had promised the "man on the moon" that we'd stay grounded in his need.

It is hard to stay grounded when you're talking about Christianity. It got very mental very early. It didn't start mental, but it got mental. Personally, I've given up asking why it did. (There are several theories.) I wish we could just go *Back to Methuselah* (G.B. Shaw), to the Sermon on the Mount, and erase the mental. But we are not the Ministry of Truth (*1984*). So I have to give a little theory. Wish I didn't, and I'll try to be brief.

The Physics of Forgiveness ("The Politics of Dancing" – Re-Flex)

Because of a conceptual requirement that God be understood as "both/and" rather than "either/or", Christian thought has bound itself to the task of working out a back story for God's engineering, or "physics", of His personal forgiveness of hard cases – of people, in other words. The way Christian thought has done this is by conceptualizing theories about how God could work things out in order that His equal qualities of justice and mercy could *both* be "satisfied" *at the same time*, with the unusual result that wayward and in fact criminal humanity could receive total pardon and therefore relief from deserved punishment.

What Christian theology came up with was a duality, and finally a Trinity, in the being of God Himself. Within this Trinity, it has often been understood that *one* part of God, i.e., the Son in God, could do justice to the *other* part of God, i.e., the Father in God, with the result that peace could be achieved – the kind of equilibrium achieved through a chemistry experiment involving the exchange of properties – in relation to His prime creation, the human race. A dangerous and creative experiment, God's Atonement in relation to Himself, had to be undertaken, because the human race was for some mysterious reason embedded with a highly resistant virus.

All the many long-standing arguments about the Trinity, not to mention the arguments about the means of Christ's Atonement to benefit man, have been in the service of a conceptual getting-our-heads-around the possibility of a complete forgiveness of the human person. The arguments were necessary, from the standpoint of logic, because of the intrinsic "unforgivability" of man due to our persistent resistance to living justly and equitably.

There was something perverse about all this exhausting argumentation. Taking a phrase from Ray Bradbury, it was a "million-year picnic". It ran straight through the entire history of Christianity. You don't see it in Jesus, which is a mighty relief. You see it in St. Paul, but with breathers when St. Paul goes back to experience. But after the New Testament was "closed", as a text I mean, then the arguments really began. When you consider the centuries! "When I think of the time gone by, I could honestly die!" ("Sue me" from *Guys and Dolls* by Frank Loesser)

Herculean theories

There are substitutionary theories of the Atonement; forensic theories about the substitution; "penal" theories within the forensic ones; completely alternative theories, known as 'Christus Victor' theories, which are anchored in myths of cosmic combat that sound almost Persian; "participationist" theories of the Atonement – "participationist" has too many syllables; "eucharistic" theories of the Atonement; and even theories of the Atonement that say there didn't need to be an Atonement in the first place. The last category of theories had direct impact on the painter Vincent van Gogh.

All of these theories are mental efforts to try to understand "What Lies Beneath" (2000) the phenomenon, which millions of people have experienced – there is no doubt about this – when they heard "the old, old story of Jesus and his love."

Many artists, and not just theologians, have tried to understand the source of the peace they have sometimes felt as a result of hearing the story. Book III of Milton's *Paradise Lost* is an impressive instance of an inspired poet trying to understand the "physics" of the Atonement. Milton goes to stupendous lengths to put into metre a lengthy "in-house" conversation in heaven, between the Son and the Father, which will result in the Son's coming to earth as a human person in order to deliver humans from themselves.

Another instance of an artistic reflection on the physics of Atonement is the metaphor of love's sacrifice that is involved in the climax of *A Tale of Two Cities* by Charles Dickens. Even the somewhat religiously neutral Shakespeare tried his hand at explaining the mechanics of mercy, near the end of *The Merchant of Venice*. The painter Albrecht Dürer wrote that his personal hold on the Atonement of Christ as explained in the writings of Martin Luther had delivered Dürer from a depression so deep that he didn't think he would ever paint another picture. The American troubadour Bob Dylan put time into the Atonement of Christ in his 1980 song, "Saved".

It is not fair for people today to dismiss all the somewhat "stretched" theories of the Atonement of Christ just because they do not like to talk about God. When you read Augustine or Pascal, or look at paintings by Rembrandt or Kerouac, who painted one Atonement (i.e., crucifixion) scene after another near the end of his life – not to mention Andy Warhol, who completely obsessed on scenes of the Last Supper during his last period of work: when you read and look at what these people did, I think you can award some "A's for effort" on the part of a lot of creative people.

And yet –

the man who is near death hasn't got time for the pain.

He is not that interested in 'Pop Art' da Vincis – they're too subtle for him now – nor does he care what exactly it was that motivated Albrecht Dürer to paint still-life hares. Does he even remember the difference between a hare and a "wabbit"? No, his eyes are dim, his ears are filled with that whooshing sound that won't go away, and his mouth is very dry.

Front story: Love's effects

Samuel Johnson said, "Depend upon it, sir, when a man knows he is to be hanged in a fortnight, it concentrates his mind wonderfully."

The English short-story writer Algernon Blackwood put the same thought in the following way: "All have some question mark, and carry it about, though with most, it rarely becomes visible until the end."[5]

---

5 Algernon Blackwood, "Descent into Egypt" in *Incredible Adventures* (London: MacMillan and Company, Limited, 1914), 255.

This guide to world religion is a homage to this thought, that the way to get to the essence of a religion is to ask what resources it has, or doesn't have, for a person at the end of his life.

Love's cause is not particularly important to a person at the end of his life. What is important is the love itself, by which the Christian religion means a forgiveness born of a one-way love from God. The mental work of building up theories to explain that love is, from the dying person's point of view, unnecessary.

Nevertheless, just as in the case of trying to understand how the Atonement worked in theory, massive efforts have gone into trying to understand how the divine revealed love that was "actualized" by means of the Atonement, works out in practice.

If I lived in a mystical vacuum, I would draw a curtain over these theories and concepts. I would do that, as I have said before, because they are mental rather than practical. They did me little good in January 2007, when my old life collapsed; and I don't think theories can do a questing world much good, either. On the other hand, they represent the subjects to which Christian thought has given its attention over many centuries. We have to look at them, at least a little, simply because the tradition of Christ's religion transmits them. For me it is a reluctant, necessary looking. From a near-death perspective, it seems extraneous. Can we at least keep it short?

"My baby must be a magician, 'cause he's sure got the magic touch" (Marvelettes)

How does love, in particular the one-way love that comes from God, actually get in play and make a difference? How does it work its magic in its target? Many who have felt "saved by the Blood of the Lamb" have wanted to go further than the experience itself, and have tried to describe the love in words.

You know how wily people, when they want to dodge a question that just requires a simple 'yes' or 'no' answer, will tell you, "Well, it's complicated."? Or they may say, "Well, you have to understand: there's a lot of history."

A lot of history! In the case of one-way love's effect on people, the history of Christian thought, which in this case involves the state of nations and vast outcomes of peoples and borders, has been very, very involved with the question of how love works. Some formal theological words for the way love works have been "justification", "law and gospel", "imputation", and *simul iustus et peccator*.

Although from the perspective of our ever-receding pro-tagonist overhead, such phrases are bound to be just words, they were not just words from the perspective of living hu-mans in the here and now of the year 1520. Those people wanted to know how they could stand – live in peace and inward quiet – in face of God's Law as decreed by Scripture and Church, not to mention the infinite smaller "laws" of human political animality. To people living in Europe in the early 1500s, let alone American people in the mid-1700s when the Great Awakening swept through the Thirteen Colonies like a viral video, it was a core question: how does

God's unconditional love act itself out in relation to my burdened and everyday mornings? Why should I get up in the morning when I'm shaky about my status should I die? In those periods of history, when childbirth was iffy and every time you took a trip, you might not come back, death was close for everyone.

Justification by Faith

To put it succinctly, Christ's love was believed to have "justified" human beings, all of whom require justification in relation to God's demand for moral perfection on their part. By "justification" was meant innocence that has been demonstrated in the face of accusation.

God's great demand for moral perfection was called, from the Bible, the Law. God's forgiveness of me, engineered by means of the "back story" of Christ's Blood-Atonement on the Cross, has justified me before God; and thus put my moral status beyond question. I can regard myself as guiltless before God as the result of Christ's Atonement.

Two Words: Law and Grace

God's love for me took two forms, it was argued from Scripture. His love was expressed in two words. These words were "Law" and "Grace". God's Law, which was intended to make my life and relationships good and equitable, was the first form of His love. The second form of it was his Grace, which set aside the accusations arising from the Law, and treated me as if I had never failed in relation to it. As an African-American Gospel song puts it, "Jesus Dropped the Charges" (The O'Neal Twins).

But how does this work in practice? How does the love that is non-accusatory, a love that has been drained completely of judgment, become effective in experience? The answer is, in formal Christian theology – or rather, in Protestant Christian theology from 1517 through to the present day – by means of *imputation*.

Imputation and analogy

Imputation is the ascription to someone of a quality they do not possess intrinsically but which the "imputer" chooses to ascribe to the "imputee" anyway. For example, you act towards a "plain Jane" or an acne-blemished and awkward young man as if they were beautiful and handsome. (They are beautiful and handsome in your eyes.) Come to find out, the acne-blemished "geek" begins to be more confident and less tentative, more sheerly "masculine", than he ever was before. And "plain Jane" begins to look pretty. Everyone can see it! She is starting to bloom. Whatever Happened to Baby Jane?

Imputation is a theological word of immense persuasion. This is because imputation happens in *life* all the time. Every time a teacher sees promise in a shy or awkward student, imputation is taking place. Every time an athletic coach begins to work with a young person who felt bashful about their body, imputation is taking place. Every time someone sees some promising quality in you that no one's ever seen in you before, least of all yourself, imputation is taking place.

From a psychological point of view, imputation is about substitute fathering and mothering. Imputation can make a decisive difference, in cases we all know and have seen –

like ourselves – between living with your tail between your legs and living with confidence and poise.

It is no wonder that Christian theologians put together their theological belief that God loves people as they are, as "sinners", with the psychic and unconscious truth that relational imputation is the main ingredient in the birth of human freedom.

As a minister, when people have said, "OK, I hear you about Christ's one-way love in ancient times and in the world of invisible truth. But tell me, how does it work now?", I have usually said back, "It works through imputation. All you need to do to understand this is "Look Around" (Sergio Mendes and Brazil '66) at people and see how they are affected by being loved." (Sergio Mendes and Brazil '66 can usually settle any argument.)

Simul iustus et peccator: Loved and human at the same time

There is a fourth word, it is actually a Latin phrase, which completes the "scheme of salvation" – love's effect – in orthodox Christian thought. Incidentally, Roman Catholicism did not consider that religion had to be as propositional, at least for the everyday Christian, as Protestantism made it.

In Protestantism there is a fourth element in this theoretical but also psychological construction. This element does not exist in Catholicism.

Because one-way love works by means of imputation, which looks on the beloved differently from the way the beloved sees himself or herself, a tension begins to build up inside the loved person. This tension is between the person who has been *seen* to be something, and the person who existed, and still exists, prior to the seeing. In the fairy tale, 'Beauty' kissed the 'Beast' and he turned into a handsome prince. He turned into the being whom he had been kissed as. He had been kissed *as if* he were a prince. But was he no longer a beast? The answer is yes and no. The same goes for the frog who was turned into a prince when the princess kissed him. Was he no longer a frog after she had kissed his slimy mouth between those bulbous eyes? The answer is yes and no.

In Christian theology the loved person is both the person he is and the person he was, although he is now going "with" the person he is. The forgiven sinner is completely forgiven – "You can't take that away from me" (George Gershwin) – but he still walks around in the body and has the memories of the man he was. The formal Latin term for this condition is *simul iustus et peccator*. It can be para-phrased as "loved and human at the same time".

The condition of being *simul iustus et peccator* carries a lot of relief when you stop and think about it. It means, I can enjoy my new position of being endearing to someone I really love and look up to – my wife, for example. At the same time I don't have to hide parts of me that haven't caught up with the person she has blessed with her affec-tion. If I believed that a person could only stay loved as long as they stayed perfect, then I would be sunk. I would be in continual conflict with my "other" self. My imputed self would exist in tension with my imperfect self-centered part, the part of me that apparently escaped the glance of my strange imputing admirer. *Simul iustus et peccator* tells the truth about me. It explains what's going on. It makes it possible for me to really "count my lucky stars": that both parts of me, the part she fell for and the part I wouldn't let be exposed to her or anyone for a million dollars, are here. I am two things at the same time, *simul iustus et peccator*.

I am Spartacus and I am also not Spartacus.

By the way, the more she imputes to me – the more of me she considers to be good even though I think it's lame – the better I seem to get. I get prettier and handsomer, smarter and more resourceful, quieter and more truthful, kinder and softer, more patient and less prone to mistakes. "And so it goes and so it goes" (Nick Lowe). The more I am loved in my unsatisfactoriness, the more satisfactory I become. This really happens.

The experience of being a person who is *simul iustus et peccator* is the practical outcome of one-way love. Knowing you are *simul iustus et peccator*, which means loved and human at the same time, quiets down the rogue child who seems to live in every person, the heedless and impish invader who even in "the best of times" (Dickens) wants you back in "the worst of times". There are those two dimensions in the life of everybody. They exist at the same time, and forever

At least until our death.

"But I've got to die tomorrow, so it really doesn't matter." (Gilbert and Sullivan, *Ruddigore*, Act Two)

The "down" side of a near-death panopticon on world religion is that it dispenses with a lot of insight that the living world needs and can use. A near-death panopticon skips over and actually discards insights that have been achieved over thousands of years. This is because the state of near death exists beyond most questions of how to conduct oneself in life. It is too late for most "answers" to apply concerning what shall I *do*. Near death superannuates ethics. As Fox Mulder, the character in "The X-Files" used to say whenever the aliens came: "All bets are off."

This is not to argue against any of the achieved answers that religions have provided to questions of personal conduct, family relationships, education of children, equity in property, laws of commerce, and the rules of social order. It is just that the near-death state of a person puts those questions in a different perspective. They are no longer questions of such urgently felt importance, although they once were. Within the "fever of life" they were important, but they are no longer. The "negative" aspect of PZ's panopticon is indifference. It's not an indifference to everything, but it is an indifference to almost everything. When you are near the point of death, you won't remember who the Steelers were or what a 'War Eagle' was. Guaranteed! But you also won't remember about your mortgage, your politics, or your father-in-law.

In the case of Christianity, the panopticon engenders an indifference to every element of the religion that does not contribute to solace for the dying person. It is Dr. Johnson's "wonderful concentration of the mind". I believe this is a hermeneutical or interpretive advantage in the study of religion, for it makes "the main thing be the main thing", which in the case of Christ's message is the unconditional forgiveness of sin. It is erasure and thereby closure. "Peace, It's Wonderful!" (Father Divine)

Curse of the Fly

There are some other themes in the message of Christ that can be of solace to the "Dying Gaul". There are insights within his message concerning the community of comfort, for example, which came to be called the church; and concerning the concrete preparation for death that every person needs in life. But some of these insights were "damaged in transit", "lost in translation", with the result that they lost their original effect. It is time to talk about transmission in religion.

Three movies were made in the late 1950s and early '60s about a scientist who had developed a machine to transmit matter from one location to another. The problem was that an insect got into the machine and was mixed up with the matter being transmitted. When the scientist tested his machine out with himself, he came out on the other end with the head of the insect rather than his own head. Conversely, the little fly got the head of the scientist. The first of the these movies was called *The Fly* and came out in 1958. The second was called *Return of the Fly* and came out in 1959. The third, which I think is the best – though it is extremely upsetting and horrible – was called *Curse of the Fly*. It appeared in 1965.

Curse of the Fly tells the alarming story of a French Canadian family, the Delambres, two sons and their father, who have taken this discovery of the transmission of matter to a whole new level: the transmission of matter overseas. They are able, through their incredible machine, to send themselves across the Atlantic Ocean. The only side-effect they have at first is extreme exhaustion.

Unfortunately, and that's a word which applies to all these *Fly* movies, there are problems in the transmission, a fly in the ointment. Down the hill from the family's mansion in Canada are little locked huts, where the poor victims of prior errors in transmission are housed, or rather, locked up. They are human monsters with misshapen, added, or subtracted limbs. They include the sons' mother and father's wife.

Fate catches up with everyone in this depressing, brilliant movie. If you see *Curse of the Fly*, you will never forget it. You will never forget the idea that errors in transmission can occur in any field of life and study, although in the movie the errors in transmission are embodied hideously.

Errors in transmission occur in religion, too. They occur because of the passage of time and because of human nature. A good ancient thing, or an excellent ancient person, becomes the object of projection on the part of people who are needy for solutions. They need solutions to the brick walls and closed doors against which they have come up in life. An ancient good is turned into something, by means of projection, that it wasn't, or wasn't quite. Add to this projection the lapse of time, and you get the religious equivalent of the poor victims of faulty transmission in *Curse of the Fly*.

Errors in transmission

Here are some examples of errors in transmission, by which a good thing in religion has been turned into something it wasn't. I describe them partly in order to underline the *virtues* they once had, or were.

We'll start with a couple of "easy" ones:

Our Father

In the days of his ministry Jesus brought a democratizing element to his movement that discouraged relationships based on status, and especially titles. Thus in Matthew 23, verse 9, he said: "Call no man your father on earth, for you have one Father, who is in heaven."

Is there any doubt what these words say?

It is wondrous that millions of Christians all around the world call their pastors "Father", and have done so for hundreds of years. In my own denomination, which is officially Protestant (i.e., its legal name includes the word "Protestant" in it) and rarely called its ministers "Father" until the late 1970s, which was the Disco Era, it is now the case that a minister is simply never *not* called "Father" if he is male. If you are ordained and wish to be called by the traditional form "Mister", you are looked upon as being a rare eccentric, and possibly a blasphemer.

This is an interesting "problem in transmission". There are many things that Jesus did not say and there are many issues to which Jesus did not address himself. But here is something Jesus *did* say: "Whatever you do, don't call any-one 'Father' as a form of religious salutation." And here we are, disobeying his express command every single day of our life in church.

What should we think about this?

Note that this almost universal contravention of Christ's imperative concerning the term "Father" prevents Christians from seeing its original meaning and therefore enjoying its original intended good effect. By vetoing the use of

"Father" for his ministers, Christ was leveling the ground of human inter-action. He was saying that we are all in the same boat. Everybody is struggling to the same degree, if not in the same way. If you are my "Father", you are superior to me and I can't relate to you as I can to my "Brother". For Christ, "Brother" was the thing, not "Father". Faulty transmission, based on some need inside people to create hierarchy, has falsified a good and freeing thing.

An across-the-board need of people to call me 'Father Paul' over 35 years of formal ministry was completely excruciating. It was a daily, sometimes hourly reminder that I was working against a feature of human nature so ingrained that there was nothing, absolutely nothing, I could do to affect it. To survive, I had to compartmentalize. But the irritation was chronic, and never went away.

Ash Wednesday

Another "whopper" of a transmission problem occurred in the case of Ash Wednesday. This one, like the evolution of "Father", is relatively minor, although it's astounding when you think about it.

About 15 years ago Episcopal churches in New York City began to notice that on Ash Wednesday they were being swamped with takers. This is to say, thousands of people were coming to Episcopal churches on Ash Wednesday to receive the imposition of ashes on their foreheads. The clergy felt flattered! People were sighted everywhere in mid-town and downtown that day, showing ashes that had been imposed by our priests. There was considerable congratulation, mingled with a little mystification, in the church press.

Although it turned out a high percentage of the people who came for ashes, especially during the lunch hour, were Roman Catholics and lapsed Roman Catholics who thought the old Episcopal churches of mid-Manhattan were Catholic churches, what interested me, and had always interested me as a minister, was that we were doing something on Ash Wednesday that was expressly forbidden by the Lord.

In the Sermon on the Mount, Christ stated that people should not display their ashes in public. This is how he put it, in Matthew 6:16-18:

"And when you fast, do not look dismal, like the hypocrites, for they disfigure their faces that their fasting may be seen by men. Truly, I say to you, they have their reward. But when you fast, anoint your head and wash your face, *that your fasting may not be seen by men* but by your Father who is in secret; and your Father who sees in secret will reward you."

Now ain't that peculiar? Christ specifically said, Don't let your practice "be seen by men". The danger of letting others see your ashes would be the danger of self-righteousness: you might begin to see yourself as superior to those who are not wearing ashes, and they in turn might begin to see you as 'holier than thou.' So the original benefit of Christ's teaching concerning public displays of signs of penitence, such as ashes, was to preserve the inwardness of religion. It is between you and God, not you and other people.

Since 1979, the year a new Prayer Book took effect, I was required to preside at Ash Wednesday services at which my parishioners expected me to impose ashes on their foreheads. It did no good whatsoever, exercised not an ounce

of persuasion, when I explained to them that such a cus-
tom was never observed in the vast majority (i.e., 90%) of
Episcopal churches prior to 1979. It didn't help me at all
when I told them how Thomas Cranmer, the first Archbishop of Canterbury of the Church of England, who was
later turned to ashes himself when he was burned at the
stake, specifically forbade the imposition of ashes on Ash
Wednesday. It was one of his first acts of reformation when
he was appointed Archbishop in 1532. Neither of these
facts did me any good. People just looked at me as if I were
crazy. ("Is our rector maybe not really religious?")

So I would try to sit it out on Ash Wednesday. I would get
another priest to impose the ashes at the altar rail while I
conducted the first part of the service and gave the sermon.
But then people would come up afterwards, at the church
door, and try to be jocular – for they liked me in general –
and say something like, "Guess our rector's taking the day
off." (Ha, Ha, Ha.) Here again, an *excruciating* aspect of
being a parish priest. At least it was only once a year.

More than ashes and titles

The problem of Ash Wednesday, which will never be cor-
rected given human nature's desire for something to "show
for it", and the problem of clergy titles, which seems to
suit both sides of the aisle, lay and ordained, are not very
important problems in the big scheme of things. They are
minor irritants in principle, although they were excruciating
to me. But they are not impossible to make peace with. You
can put up with them if you have a sense of humor and can
occasionally say 'no' out of respect for yourself. ("Dammit! I
am Mr. Zahl. Haven't you ever read *Adam Bede*?") But they

are issues which are not remotely decisive for a person who is near death. No one I know who has been near death has ever told me they were worried about clergy nomenclature or Ash Wednesday displays in mid-town.

But there are two *other* problems of transmission that have actually set back the ability of Christianity to give aid and comfort to the dying. These problems have damaged the religion's ability to draw upon its greatest strength, "Mama's Pearl" (Jackson 5) of great price. These two problems of transmission relate to the organized church and to a person's preparation for death.

The Kingdom of God among the near-dead: May 28, 1453

The purpose of the church in Christianity is to be a fellowship of comforters, friends, and helpers in order to aid human beings in the difficult task of negotiating life's challenges on their own. Without the accompaniment of "fellow travelers", life is too hard for most people. It is also impossible to bear at the end.

Sadly, and few would deny this today, the church of Christ rarely is what it is supposed to be, and rarely acts as it is supposed to act. It is more typically an institution that resembles other institutions, like colleges, political parties, and hospitals, although it is slower to adapt than many businesses, and strangely more harsh in relation to offenders within it.

But wait:

I wish to show to the near-dead the very good thing that we usually miss from the church. Church can be good, although it rarely is.

In Mika Waltari's novel *The Dark Angel*, he describes the last Christian service that was ever held in the Church of St. Sophia in Constantinople. It was held on the night of May 28, 1453, hours before the final assault on the city by the Ottoman Turks, during which almost all the people who gathered in the church that night would be killed, raped, or sold into slavery the following day.

Here is Waltari's description of the service, in which Roman Catholics and Greek Orthodox, who had previously been in violent conflict over a phrase in the Nicene Creed, laid down their differences and received the Eucharist together and for the last time[6]:

> "We rode together to the church as day was fading behind the Turkish camp and shedding a last gleam of blood on the green domes of the churches. ... In my heart I knew that for the last time a doomed Byzantium was gathering to dedicate itself to death.

> "... In the presence of death, all quarreling, suspicion and hatred disappeared. Each and everyone bowed his head before the inscrutable mystery, according to his own conscience.

> "In the presence of us all the Emperor confessed his sins in the phrases that centuries have hallowed. The Latins joined with him in murmuring chorus. ... tonight no one was disturbed by these divergences. All proceeded as by tacit agreement, and the Greeks in their relief wept more loudly than before, because their faith was no longer contemned.

> "There were so many in the church that the bread would not go around. But each one willingly shared with his

---

6 Mika Waltari, *The Dark Angel*. Translated by Naomi Walford (New York: G.P. Putnam's Sons, 1953), 322-323.

nearest neighbors the morsel he had received, so that
all who came might have at least a crumb of the sacred
Body of Christ. Whether the bread were leavened or
unleavened made no difference now.

"During the service, which lasted several hours, we were
moved by a strong and radiant ecstasy, more wonderful
than any I have known in any church."

"In the presence of death": that is the key phrase. In the
presence of death, the animating purpose of church that
night became, and still becomes, clear: mystery, tolerance,
compassion, even ecstasy and out-of-body feeling. No vertical status, no hollow "cant", no empty ritual (but real ritual, which means something to people), no judgments and
no opinions. Rather, practical aid in time of need, mutual
support, forgiveness, and encouragement.

When, after almost 40 years since I was ordained, I compare
church that night in 1453 with church as I have known it
institutionally, I laugh a little. But I also cry. It could have
been so good.

Emil Brunner, a Swiss theologian who died in 1966, stated
what has been and what may be. I think Brunner said it for
our time[7]:

> "Not the hostility of the unbelieving world, but clerical
> parsonic ecclesiasticism has ever been the greatest ene-
> my of the Christian message and of brotherhood rooted
> in Christ... We must therefore be prepared for the pos-
> sibility that it might be the will of God eventually to
> destroy the ancient churchly framework of the *Ecclesia*."

---

7 *The Misunderstanding of the Church*. Translated by Harold Knight (Philadelphia:
The Westminster Press, 1953), 117-119.

Eschatology

Ernst Käsemann was a New Testament scholar who said that apocalyptic is the mother of all Christian theology. What Käsemann meant was this: the conviction the early Christians had that Christ was soon to come back to the world, after he had left it following his resurrection from the dead, forced them, when he didn't come back, to "theologize" about why. If the early Christians had not believed in the imminent return of Christ during their lifetimes, then they wouldn't have had to come up with explanations of why he was delayed. Their "apocalyptic", which means the picture they had of his swift rebound to a visible conquest, made it so his delay had to be rationalized.

Eschatology is a term in academic theology for the "end times" of life and for what religious people have to say concerning life's conclusion. In Islam, the Day of Resurrection will judge every person for everything they have ever done. Many will go to heaven, and many will go to hell. Islamic eschatology also invites martyrs to a delightful heaven of buzzing gardens and voluptuous maidens. Jewish eschatology talks more about your ending as being embodied in the lives of your children here, in this world not the next, in whom your memory will be preserved. Most forms of Judaism also include the element of waiting for the Messiah of Israel to come.

The eschatology of Hinduism is connected with the requirement that we dis-connect from our karma, which is our current destiny as affected by our past lives, and from the enforced reincarnations to come, by getting off the wheel of repetition in favor of dis-attachment from the world and dissolution into the Brahman, or transcendent Reality. Buddhism has an eschatology similar to its "mother-religion", Hinduism, although the end-point of Buddhism is a mostly formless negation. In practice, Buddhism can be *anti*-eschatological because it locates ultimacy in the present.

In Christian theology the early Christians were confused by certain things that Christ had said toward the end of his life. They had also been brought up in the idea that the Messiah of Israel was coming. The Messiah was coming into real time, and would have the authority as well as the power to change the world in the cause of Israel. At the time of Christ it was believed by many Jews that the Messiah was coming imminently.

It is not surprising that the early Christians began to teach the Second Coming of Christ. Later on, as time elapsed, the Second Coming of Christ had to be "diverted", we could almost say sublimated, into teachings about Christ's Presence in the Eucharist, or in the visible Church of Rome (and Constantinople), or in sacred paintings called "icons", or, for Protestants later, in the written words of the Holy Bible.

For Christian political activists the Second Coming of Christ was identified with a more just society. That is what the "Diggers" believed in England during the mid-1600s. Where was Christ to be found, since he was thought with unquestionable authority to have said he was coming back? You had to locate him somewhere, "else your faith was in vain" (I Corinthians 15:14).

Whatever the actual truth is concerning the return of Christ to this planet, it is not doing much for our man on the ceiling. It doesn't matter much to him when and whether Christ returns to the place that he himself is in the process of leaving. It might be nice for him to know that his children or grand-children will have the experience of seeing Christ face to face within their own histories. But at this point in *his* history, it doesn't matter very much what will transpire later on down below. He is beyond that now. To tell you the truth, he was beyond that when he first started having chest pains.

If only the transmission of eschatology had not been complicated by obscure or obscurely remembered statements made by Jesus. If only the apocalyptic mood of subjugated Israel at the time had not issued in such immediate and vivid longings. If only!

What our hero *could* use, however, is more honesty and less denial concerning the subject of physical death. No one would ever talk to him about that when he was down *there*. It was a taboo subject.

Ikiru

Have you seen the movie *Ikiru*, directed by Akira Kurosawa? It came out in 1952 in Japan but didn't become well known in the West until several years after its release.

Ikiru, which means "to live" in English, tells the story of an "everyman", 'Watanabe', who contracts stomach cancer. But no one will tell him he has stomach cancer. Even the doctors lie to him. Fortunately, you might say, he knows. He just does. But everyone around him equivocates, from his son to his son's wife to his colleagues at the office.

The man in *Ikiru* has to face the eschatological fact of his own death completely alone. That he does so at all is a miracle.

One of the main purposes of a religion

Christ told many parables about people who are caught unawares by death. We are characteristically unprepared for death. Christ said the end would come like a thief in the night, when you least expect it.

One of the main purposes of a religion, any religion, is to help people come to terms with the mystery of death. At the very least, a religion should support a person in asking the question, let alone enduring the experience. A headline in "The Onion" newspaper read, "Poll Reveals Mortality Rate Still Holding at 100%". When the transmission of Christ's emphasis on the need to prepare for death is turned into a telescope gazing out at something speculative, like the time and place of Christ's possible return, that is a tragedy. It is a major lost opportunity, caused by a vital insight's having been diverted from its main course into a tributary.

Several emphases in Christian life and thought over the centuries can be explained as problems of transmission. Did he really mean *that*, or *this*? Did people's need to think a thing overwhelm the original statement? The original insight, like the poor Canadian father in *Curse of the the Fly*, is somewhere over the Atlantic, scrambled into a thousand pieces, never to be put back together again.

The Jesus-Prayer

In his novel *Franny and Zooey*, which was published in 1961, J.D. Salinger has 'Franny', Salinger's hero, try to explain to her college boyfriend the meaning of the 'Jesus Prayer'. The 'Jesus-Prayer', which comes from the Eastern Orthodox tradition of Christianity, consists of the words, "Jesus Christ, Son of God, have mercy on me, a sinner."

Startling as it can be to first-time readers of Salinger's famous novel, the focus of the "Franny" section of *Franny and Zooey* is on the central idea of the Christian religion.

J.D. Salinger understood that his character's near-obsession with the 'Jesus-Prayer' comes out of her psychic need and condition. It is not a fully rational interest, if there really is such a thing. Franny *needs* what she takes to be the meaning of the Prayer.

This section of our panopticon is ready to end. It was not intended to be a complete guide to Christianity. How would that be possible, given the length, breadth, and depth of the tradition?

What this was meant to be was a short course in what a dying person can use, right on the spot – 'X' marks the spot – of his final departure. If I cannot use what I hear and see there and then, then it must be secondary. If I cannot use an insight at that point, even if it was pleasing in itself and interesting when I was involved in physical life, then it must, deep down, be immaterial. The Trinity is a splendid and even magnificent approach to the mystery of God; but *As I Lay Dying* (William Faulkner), it is too complicated for me. Questions related to predestination or the cause of evil in the world are important questions. But they don't mean much when I am past explanations and living purely in the realm of simple touch, impaired hearing, and dimming image.

No, what I need is peace so that I can go on. And the only way I can have peace is if I can get this goddamned burden of my past off my back, this movie in my mind, which gives me unending grief with its re-winding reel-to-reel of personal failures and self-centeredness.

What I mostly need right now is what J.D. Salinger gave his character 'Franny' in his novel:

"Jesus Christ, Son of God, have mercy on me, a sinner."

T-Rex

The greatest gift to the world of the Christian religion, which comes straight from its founder, is the gift of absolving sacrificial love. This is the gift of mercy. Whatever words are right to describe what he did, he regarded his life, in all the Gospel biographies of him, as something lived "for you".

How little you meet in people a desire to do something "for you", i.e., for a person who is not oneself. Unselfishness is rarely found. Lots of times when you think a person is being unselfish, you find out later that their action or speech was really designed to advance themselves. It's disappointing about people when you find this out, but you often do. So when you come up against unselfishness that is sincere, it is so striking – "Bang a Gong" (T-Rex) – that it has the effect of inspiring life-long marriages and life-long loyalties. Sincere unselfishness, "Mama's Pearl", creates partnerships of trust and contracts of steel.

At the end of Federico Fellini's movie *La Strada* (1954), the main character, who has acted like a brute, finds out how much his diminutive and almost dim-witted wife really loved him. He goes down to the beach, sits down on the sand, puts his head on his knees, and sobs with the great energy of his over-sized body. The giant brute's been tamed, by a love that's real.

But there's more: there is hope for the brute.

There is also hope for the poor soul who is floating over-head, as his life ebbs out on the surgical table below. You can put a line through the past. As William Inge said in a Christian vein, "Death makes us all innocent." This is the core of it. The guilt and sorrow, desperate wrenching sorrow and regret, that is universal to all selves, is erased by "have mercy on me, a sinner". This is why I was not with-out hope when I used to visit the dying, from Tarrytown to Anniston. I am still not without hope. And now it's me.

"Behind the Music" (VH 1)

> "... for the first time, very dimly, I caught glimpses of an extraordinary figure moving behind the inaccuracies, contradictions and propaganda of the gospel story."[8]

There is hope for Christianity.

But it does not lie with the church.

This is an old insight and not a particularly happy one if you are a Christian. It has been stated again and again, by good people. Dostoyevsky said it in such a way that you

---

8   Christopher Isherwood, *Diaries Volume One: 1939-1960.* Edited and introduced by Katherine Bucknell (London: Vintage, 1997), 187.

could say it was said for all time, in the "Grand Inquisitor" section of *The Brothers Karamazov*.

I like the way Woody Guthrie said it, in 1940:

> "When Jesus come to town, all the working folks around
> Believed what he did say
> But the bankers and the preachers, they nailed Him on
>   the cross,
> And they laid Jesus Christ in his grave."

The bankers and the preachers!

There never has been room for him in the inn. Sometimes I think we need to stop looking for him there.

Robert Nathan was an American writer who was not a Christian. But he wrote sympathetically about Christians. Today Robert Nathan is remembered because of his novel *The Bishop's Wife*, published in 1928, which was later made into a famous movie starring Cary Grant, David Niven, and Loretta Young. *The Bishop's Wife* was re-made in 1996 and this time called *The Preacher's Wife*. It had an African-American setting.

But Robert Nathan wrote more than just *The Bishop's Wife*.

In 1931 he wrote a novel called *There Is Another Heaven*. It concerns a place where conservative Protestant Christians find themselves after death. It is an upsetting read if you "are or ever have been a member of..." But it also has an upbeat insight, an insight that is good for this guide to world religion.

At a certain point during their period of residence in "Another Heaven", some of the dead begin to notice something:

they never see Jesus. They attend all manner of sanctifying functions and religious exercises, and are certainly provided for in every regular way. But a few of them start to ask a troubling question: "Where is Jesus? I haven't seen Jesus yet." *There is Another Heaven* is a little like an episode of *The Twilight Zone.*

Robert Nathan's short answer in his book is that Jesus is not there. This is the shocking but true guess on the part of a recently arrived character. The response Nathan has his character make to his correct surmise is dramatic and moving. It is also hopeful.

Just because the church is not the place to look for Christ does not mean that he is not worth looking for. To the contrary! The future of Christianity consists in the search, right now, for that "damned elusive Pimpernel" (Baroness Orczy). And when Christ gets found – and he will not be found in such a way that he can be pinned down – my own religion will not be a religion any more, or what modern skeptics like to call a "belief system". No, it will be a connection, with reality.

The "extraordinary figure" that Isherwood began to think about when he was doing refugee relief work among the Quakers of Philadelphia during the Second World War, a figure whom Isherwood had hated because of his relation in Isherwood's mind to the kind of Christianity he had been taught in prep school and by his mother – that figure is the hope for my religion.

The problem of St. Paul

I used to put my weight on the teachings of St. Paul, and especially on St. Paul's teachings concerning the futility of human works and the alternative of God's Grace that covers them all by means of a blessed amnesia. Paul's de-construction of our compulsive human projects to self-justify and self-improve still seems uniquely insightful.

But the more you study St. Paul, the more you see that he says a lot of things, and that his teachings are full of tension. By "tension" I do not mean torture. By tension, I mean that St. Paul was coming from a complex personal past into a complex and unfamiliar new world of new peoples and new beliefs. There is a kind of torque to Paul's thought that spins off shavings in more than one direction. Sometimes you can take what he says in different ways.

He stated himself that his mission made him try to become "all things things to all men" (I Corinthians 9:22).

There are "Catholic" turns in Paul and "Protestant" ones. There are "mystic" ways in Paul; and worldly, possibly even duplicitous ways in Paul. He is not a completely clear stream. That is because he couldn't be. Because he was the only Christian he knew in most of the places he went, he had to adapt what he said to very different audiences. This is why his message, although it positively overflows with insights, is not one thing.

The future of Christianity may not lie with St. Paul. Certainly the future of Christianity is with Jesus.

I don't think St. Paul would mind me saying that!

What Jesus taught and did

Jesus has been a victim of history, or rather, ancient historiography, in that four biographies of him were composed by different writers using different sources. It has been a pet project of scribes and scholars to try and produce a "harmony of the gospels" that would resolve or reconcile the inconsistencies that divide the four gospels from each other in their portraits of Christ.

No one has ever succeeded in reconciling the differences among the gospels. They will be there 'til the end of time.

But you don't have to give up the search. There are some "Lines, Angles and Rhymes" (The 5th Dimension) in the story of his life. There are "bare necessities" (*The Jungle Book*, 1967) about him, and they are not superficial things.

What are the bare necessities of Jesus' life? What did he teach and what did he do?

First, Jesus said to people that they needed to repent. By "repent" he meant what Bob Dylan meant when he sang, "Gotta change my way of thinking". It seems obvious from the condition of the world in general and my chaotic life in particular that something's got to change.

Recently I was sitting in the barber shop awaiting my turn. I happened to look up from my magazine, and there was a mirror. I was appalled by what I saw: unbrushed white hair and a sprouting cowlick, like 'Alfalfa' in *The Little Rascals*; a four-days' beard, which looked awful; my stretched belt just making it around my waist; an ancient Lacoste t-shirt with a central spot of jam on it from a Müller's yogurt; and a growing paunch in the center of it all. Had Jesus walked by the barber shop that minute and I'd seen him through the window, I would have followed him immediately! Jesus told the truth about the impossibility of controlling our psychic, cosmetic, and social environment.

"Get out of Sour Milk Sea, / You don't belong there." (George Harrison)

SECOND, he healed people's psychic illnesses, and sometimes their physical ones, by separating the person from the disease. The term for this at the time was exorcism. Jesus was a psychological healer. This does not exhaust the healings he performed, but for the current age, we all have psychological illnesses.

Instead of a "personal trainer", I am currently lobbying for a personal healer. Jesus was one. What he did was not superstitious or magical, in my view. He got inside the inner conflicts of the mind, and the people he delivered usually ended up following him.

THIRD, he taught that the root problem of human nature is inward, not outward. The conflicts of the mind that can make a person's life hell are psycho-genetic. "I have met the enemy and he is us" (Pogo).

Ethics, which is the science of 'what shall I do?', concerns motives rather than actions. Don't go west, young man (Horace Greeley) – go in.

FOURTH, human nature is extremely disturbed. The archaeology of ill will and anxiety is deep and multi-layered. The disturbance involved in being a human being, even under the best conditions of having relatively non-neurotic parents, is so troubling that the alternatives can be as stark as suicide or salvation. There are uncontrollable inner elements in almost everybody. At the darkest hour, and you have probably had one, we need to be saved, and that is not exaggerating.

Fifth, compassion is everything. Jesus not only taught this but he practiced it. He was like "Allah the Compassionate, the Merciful". But he also had "Love's Body" (Norman O. Brown) and seemed to the people he met to actually be compassion.

Those are the five broad strokes of what I think is possible to say concerning the essence of Jesus.

The only person in the world

In 2003 I wrote the following paragraph to try and sum up Jesus. As if! Yet I still believe what I wrote, and am amazed, given what happened in 2007, that I still do[9]:

> "Jesus was the First Christian, whose discontinuities were the seed of his universal interest and aptness. This was because of his astonishing will to say one thing: Repent, everyone, for you cannot save your far-gone selves. I have come for you as if you in your miredness were the only person in the world."

Judaism

It is hard for a non-Jew today, and especially for a Christian non-Jew, even a very "liberal" Christian, to speak about Judaism, for fear of being told: "Who gave you the right? Given the tragic history of the Jewish people, and the security situation of the State of Israel, what gives any Christian the right to make judgments about Judaism? See where that led in the past!"

---

9   Paul F. M. Zahl, *The First Christian* (Grand Rapids, Michigan/Cambridge, U.K.: William B. Eerdmans Publishing Company, 2003), 127.

Recently, a public official in Israel got into trouble, though fairly mild trouble, for writing on the internet, in response to a "white paper" from the Church of Scotland to the effect that the "Land" of Israel should be interpreted "spiritually" rather than "geo-politically": "Do Israelis give a flying f___ what the Church of Scotland thinks?"

On the one hand, this made me laugh. I mean, from a certain point of view, who amongst us does "give a flying f___ what the Church of Scotland thinks"?

But seriously, I took his comment to heart, and think I understand where he was coming from. People do not like to be lectured, especially if the lecturer is presuming to use your religion, and it is not theirs, to lecture you. As a Christian I am reluctant to say anything about Judaism that is not completely positive.

I would add that an "outsider" can sometimes appreciate aspects of a religion that the "insider" takes for granted.

Floating on the ceiling as I am right now, reaching all around me with rapid-eye-movement for anything I can hold onto, there are two incomparable strengths of Judaism with which a Gentile like me can identify and from which I desire to learn.

Good fathers (and close families)

The first of these incomparable strengths of Judaism is this one:

Judaism produces great Dads.

One of the first things I noticed in secondary school and college, and one of the first things I noticed when later

I became a father myself, is that career, or the supposed demands of one's career, had the ability, within the families of almost all my friends, to supersede the responsibilities of fatherhood. I knew few sons of fathers whose fathers did not give first place in their allotment of time to their careers. The sons of these fathers were in effective second place when it came to the allotment of their fathers' time. This was true of my own father, and it was true of my friends' fathers. There were a few exceptions, but not many. We would usually gravitate emotionally to those fathers of our friends who were the exceptions.

Then one day I was invited to the home of a boy who was of the Jewish faith. (Most of my friends came from semi-observant Protestant families of one sort or another.) When I walked in the door of my new friend's house, the first thing I noticed was that his parents had converted a whole room of their house into a gym for basketball. And it didn't feel at all like parental pressure.

My friend was not a great athlete. But he did like basketball ("She Likes Basketball" - *Promises, Promises*). What it was, what I was seeing when I went in the front door of his house, was joy! The father of that house was showing his son, in a dazzling way to me, that his son's love of basketball was now a love that his father shared. There was a oneness between father and son, a shared love of whatever the son chose to love, which was totally new to me. It was as if the father were proving his love to the child rather than the child having to prove his love to the father. I observed a kind of joy in his son, on the part of the father, which combined unquestioned acceptance of his son's interests with active support of them.

Many years later, I saw a documentary about the cinematographer Haskell Wexler. It is called *Tell Them Who You Are* and was released in 2004. In this documentary, which was directed by Haskell Wexler's son Mark, it was explained that when Haskell Wexler as a young man showed an interest in movie photography, his father gave Haskell Wexler enough money to start a studio and make his own movie. To my friend's father and to Haskell Wexler's father, such gestures seemed like they were standard operating procedure. To me and to almost all my other friends, living as we were in the shadow of some important 'Willy Loman' or other, they were awesome and Homeric.

Such encouragement of a son by his father, this unconditional "all in", I rarely saw in Gentile homes, not to mention my own. I envied my friend.

I saw this again in college, where almost all my friends who were of the Jewish faith had extremely supportive fathers – the girls as well as the boys. The support they were receiving felt like this, although the words are mine: "Because you are my child, I am totally on your side. You don't have to do a thing to convince me of anything. I love you simply because you are my son. Period. You can therefore count on me completely. What is more, this is what I'll do..."

That is the kind of unconditional support that results in close families. It is a rock on which you can stand when you are growing up, and it gets passed on through you, almost without trying.

I have conducted hundreds of Christian funerals. You would not believe how many of them have involved fractured families. And when I say fractured, I mean fractured:

three sons not attending their father's funeral and he had four children;

a son not attending his father's funeral, and then two years later not attending his mother's funeral;

and once, one grown son throwing another grown son into their father's grave during the interment.

Twice I have conducted funerals in which a uniformed armed guard was present. The reason?:

to prevent one of the relatives from getting violent in relation to the other relatives during the service.

All these things really happened! I was there.

Only once did I conduct a Christian funeral when the adult sons spoke of their father, the deceased, the way I had heard Jewish friends of mine speak of their fathers. I was dazzled. It was the only service of its kind and tone that I ever conducted. It was in a suburban Episcopal church.

"We who are ... Gentile sinners", to quote the Book of Galatians, are much more likely to have fathers who come out of *Death of a Salesman*. These men are possessed by their (crummy) careers! All they do is work, all they seem to want to do is work. And for what? So they can retire to Vero and have a heart attack?

Judaism seems to be in the business of creating good fathers, fathers who put being a father first over almost every other task of life. I think Judaism is in the business of creating close families. How could an outsider not look at this with admiration, and envy?

Chances are that poor old Floater up on the ceiling – it's too late for him in the paternal function of his life – had an absent father.

The Colossus of New York

In 1958 a movie was released called *The Colossus of New York*. At the climax of the movie, a ten-foot-tall robot with partly human features goes berserk in the entrance hall of the United Nations. Behind the robot, who is the 'Colossus of New York', you can see, as he goes berserk and shoots disintegration-rays from his electric eyes, a text from the Bible that is chiseled on the wall. For the audience this was probably intended to be a "teaching moment", though at the time I was much more interested in the disintegration-rays coming out of the eyes of the Colossus.

The text behind the 'Colossus of New York' came from Isaiah, chapter two, verse four:

"And he shall judge among the nations, and shall rebuke many people: and they shall beat their swords into plow-shares, and their spears into pruning hooks: nation shall not lift sword against nation, neither shall they learn war any more."

I think this movie juxtaposition of robot with Prophet is wonderful. It also illustrates another unsurpassed element in Hebrew religion: the prophetic word of humanity to our inhumanity, a word from God to the anger and ill will of men.

In the ancient world, Rome as a world-power – as the world-power – very rarely closed the Gate of Janus. The Gate of Janus, a symbolic gate, had to stay open at all times when Rome was at war. As long as there was a military campaign going on anywhere, in any province of the Empire, the Gate of Janus had to stay open. And because Rome was at war almost all of the time, the Gate was almost always open. Not until the reign of the Emperor Augustus was the gate closed for any long period of time. Under Augustus the Gate was actually mostly closed. That is why they called his reign the "Pax Romana".

This points to the never-ending story of constant warfare in the history of the world. It is "a tale told by an idiot" (Macbeth) and can't ever seem to draw to an end. There is not even a "Pax Americana" to compete with the ancient "Pax Romana" under Augustus. America seems to be always at war.

Which is why, when I watch *The Colossus of New York*, I think I am in touch with something important. The people who made that movie knew that their ten-foot-tall robot would not survive if he were exposed to the pacific message on the United Nations wall. You could guess that pretty soon after the 'Colossus' shambles – I love the word "shambles" – to a point just in front of Isaiah, chapter two, verse four, he is probably going to fall down dead. It is all a symbol, but still a powerful one.

To pick out Isaiah 2:4 is almost arbitrary. The message of Isaiah can also be found in Jeremiah and Ezekiel, Hosea and Jonah, Micah and Habakkuk, and Malachi. And in several other places in the Hebrew Prophets.

When I read the Hebrew Prophets, I read the universal voice of prophecy. It is the touching cry of all peoples in favor of justice and of peace. As a Gentile Christian, I am both skewered and strengthened by the Prophets. When I visit the Boston Public Library and view "The Hebrew Prophets" by the painter John Singer Sargent, I am touched down to my toes. I especially like it when it's cold and drizzly outside, so the warmth of their breath, the Prophets' inspired breath, touches my cheeks and turns them red.

Hardest thing I ever had to do

I was required to learn Biblical Hebrew as a pre-condition of beginning a doctoral dissertation at Tübingen in 1992. Because I was over 40 and had to learn it through another foreign language, it was the hardest thing I ever had to do in university life. But there was a pay-off.

The pay-off was that I was examined in the Book of Micah.

I had to learn how to read Micah in Hebrew. Even though I knew about Hebrew prophecy in theory, and even though I had stood in the very spot where 'The Colossus of New York' learned his lesson, I really knew nothing about the Prophets. And then I read Micah in Hebrew.

We all know these things in our own languages, some of them unspoken. But here is one again: "He has showed you, O man, what is good; and what does the Lord require of you but to do justice, and to love kindness, and to walk humbly with your God" (Micah 6:8).

"It's Too Late" (Carole King)

But what about our "upstairs" friend, transfixed half-way, you might say, between heaven and hell? Do the Hebrew Prophets speak to him? Can they lend him some aid, "now and in the hour of my death"? Probably not, in fact.

It seems too late for the Prophets to help him. Before he got sick and ended up on a steel operating table, he could have used them, he could have really used them. A lot of things in his life, especially the conflicts he had with his children and also with his former wife, their mother, would have improved if he had listened to Isaiah and Micah. He would have done well for himself to turn his spears into pruning hooks – personally, I mean. But that he didn't do, and he didn't understand that he should. So his arteries started getting clogged and he "arrested". It's probably too late for his doctors to save him. What is he going to do?

I wish

Judaism is the mother of the great religions of the West. It is one of the greatest of all religions. Neither Christianity nor Islam would exist if it were not for Judaism.

The Jewish religion has given to the West, and to any country or region of the world where Jews have worshipped God and settled, an essential quality of fathering and family life, to sons and daughters, which is the wonder of our planet. I wish I had been born a Jew.

Judaism has also given to the world the limitless voice of the Hebrew Prophets. Never has their word been more needed, although many who ought to be listening are not. I wish I could have sat with Jeremiah after his City was gone, and "watched the skies" with Micah. I wish I could actually hear what they heard, in the way they heard it. But I can read it, and "mark" it; and learn it.

This world

One further thought: Judaism in general is a religion of this world. That is to say, it has a lot to say to the living. It is for the 'now' of life and the 'here' of life. It understands about fathers and sons, and daughters and fathers, and the atomic energy for good that is fostered in close families. It works! Gentile dads ought to sit on the ground these days, throw ashes on their heads, and plead to their Jewish neighbors:

"How do you do it?! Tell us how you do it!"

Moreover, Gentile Presidents of the United States, together with their Cabinets and advisers, ought to say nothing, and do nothing, until they have scheduled 96 hours of Torah study on the subject of war and peace. Then maybe, just maybe...

But wait a minute, I can still hear our friend. He seems to be upside-down now, and he's tapping something out. Damn, the ceiling's made of cork! You can barely hear what he's tapping.

Oh!: It's S. O. S.

Islam

Islam is a world religion, now the second most populous after Christianity, that has something important to offer the dangling man. It also has a lot to offer people in the prime of their lives. For people in the prime of their lives, and especially people who live in families, Islam offers an alternative, through its Five Pillars of religious practice, to the exhaustion and fever of life in the Western world.

The dangling man, by the way, is beyond alternatives, as good as they may be, to that fever of life, because he is already dying of "Western"-style stress. He might have lived to 100 if he'd adopted Islam. And we haven't even gotten to Buddhism yet.

But Islam still has something important to give our actor in his one-man show, his swan song. Islam is a certain way of seeing: oneness rather than many-ness. This is a supreme feature of the religion, and it did not get garbled in transmission.

Islam recognized the transmission problem

Early in its history Islam recognized the transmission problem affecting religion. The Prophet Muhammad discerned that Adam, Noah, Abraham, Moses, and Jesus had all been bearers of revelation. He gave them credit as prophets of the mighty way. But Muhammad also said that none of these figures had been interpreted with complete accuracy. They were bearers of religious truth but had all been misunderstood. It wasn't their fault that they had been misunderstood. It was the fault of "the parishioners"!

Muhammad believed that he had been given the right lens, the Qu'ran, to understand his predecessors in the Word of God; and that this lens, given him directly by the Angel Gabriel, was not obscured by human misunderstandings. Muhammad presented his revelation as complete and therefore final. The medium and the message were now the same.

The loneliest number

A friend of ours was recently extremely ill. He was in acute care for four weeks. He said later that during the entire time he couldn't read, couldn't watch TV, could barely speak, couldn't think even. At the same time he couldn't sleep, that is, without sedation; and couldn't stay still, again without sedation. He didn't mind visitors, although he hated the frequent visits from his nurses to take blood and from his doctors to feel his wounds. Looking back on his ordeal, our friend says he wouldn't wish what he went through on his worst enemy.

This is a little what it's like for a nearly dead person. He can't stay still, but nor does moving around afford him relief. This is also why a state of being near death is a good panopticon for looking at religion. In order to have an impact on that extremely uncomfortable state of personal *extremis*, the song of religion has to be short and soft.

Islam has just such a song to sing to the dying. It is only One Thing. Islam testifies that God is One. Oneness is not just an attribute of God; it is *the* attribute of God. You could almost say that Oneness is the governing attribute of life. Everything we see depends for its life and outcome on the One God, and there is nothing that doesn't.

This insight endows Islam with a very high doctrine of Providence: Everything is written and has been written, and is in the hands of God yesterday, today, and forever. Nothing is removed from God, untouched by God, or unconnected with God.

Islam's idea of God is monist rather than dualist.

Islam's monism can be explained partly by the Prophet's view that Christianity's teaching of the Triune God was tritheist. Muhammad reacted against the way Christian theology had turned the One God of Hebrew thought into a being that came in three Persons. It is hard to imagine how a religious inquirer living at that time, when militant schools of thought within Christianity made people willing to die for verbal formulas concerning the Trinity, would not have heard Muhammad's message as a breath of fresh air.

My friend wanted to know nothing as he lay in the ICU during his illness. Or at least nothing except a sure smile and three little words. He did not want the Many, he wanted the One, which is to say, he wanted present love. He wanted the Substance underneath the form, the thing signified and not the sign. And everything in shorthand.

It is impossible to overstate the oneness that governs Islam. Everything is permeated by it. Religions have a tendency to compartmentalize. This is because *people* have a tendency to compartmentalize. It is natural to cordon off parts of your life from other parts. Unreality thrives on compartments. Islam, too, because it is a religion made up of people, shows compartments. But not in principle! Therefore less in practice. Western people are both undone and intrigued by the atmosphere of religious acceptance and humility that permeates Muslim cultures. T.E. Lawrence succumbed to it, for example. Cat Stevens, too.

I thought it was interesting that when it came time for a Hollywood-style movie to be made about the Prophet Muhammad, they hired an Irish Protestant, H.A.L. (Harry) Craig, to write the script. It was called *The Message* and was released in 1976.

Harry Craig grew up in Clonlara vicarage and knew about the Old Religion (Protestant) of clear glass, no altar cross and a high pulpit. I have been to Church of Ireland parishes that almost resemble mosques, with little or nothing between the individual person and the Message, or rather, between the individual person and God in Person. There is a strain in world religion that wants no frills. It suspects frills. It is not surprising that when the Ottoman Turks captured Constantinople on May 29, 1453, the first thing they officially did was to turn Saint Sophia into a Presbyterian church.

K.I.S.S. (Keep It Simple, Stupid.)

The Five Pillars of Islam

Although it's a little late for a man in the grip of a fatal illness to change his life, he could have done a lot worse than to embrace the Five Pillars of Islam. Had he done so, chances are he would not be in the fix he is, at least not yet. Maybe he wouldn't be saying to his prior life what Oliver Hardy used to say to Stan Laurel: "Well, it's a fine mess you've gotten us into this time." All Stan could ever do was cry.

We were in Morocco and one of our friends was a religiously skeptical Episcopalian. We were having lunch on the deck of an excellent seaside restaurant, when an old man suddenly appeared on the rocks below us, near where the waves were breaking. He unrolled a prayer rug and started to pray. It was noon, "Sweet Hour of Prayer". Our friend the religious skeptic said, "If Christians were like *that*, I might be one now." Like the rest of us there, sitting outside and looking out to sea, she was touched by the old man.

Two things I think it was that touched her: the humility of his action and his unselfconsciousness. I don't believe the man realized for a second that he was being watched. After he completed his prayers, he rolled the rug back up, walked to our right over the rocks, and disappeared. I have a feeling he is still alive. That kind of humility helps you live longer.

The Five Pillars of religious practice in Islam are:

TESTIMONY, which is a believer's one-time public declaration that Allah is the only God and Muhammad is His Prophet;

PRAYER five times per day, like the old man and the sea;

ALMS-GIVING to the poor and the disabled;

FASTING, especially during the holy month of Ramadan; and

PILGRIMAGE, which is the journey to Mecca, the City of the Prophet.

The Five Pillars of Islam build a kind of wall around you. When they are connected to a happy family, to your life at home if it is happy – and I think it would be hard not to be happy if you lived the Five Pillars – the wall around you is secure.

You can find this out for yourself by visiting a Muslim family almost anywhere in the world. In the most crowded city or the most remote outpost, when you are invited into the home of an observant family, you will be amazed at the discontinuity between the world outside and the world inside. You may have had to go down a crowded street and into a dirty entry-way, but when you walk in the door, Presto! There's a thick wall-to-wall carpet, sound-insulating hangings on the clean white walls, framed pretty pictures up and down those walls, lovely curtains over the windows, and then they serve you tea in salvers like you can buy on Madison Avenue. The family bond is air-tight – sometimes too tight for Westerners. It is absolute, in other words. "I have this cousin-in-law", they will tell you, "twice removed. But he wants to go to America. Can you help get him a visa?" You say to yourself, "Cousin-in-law twice removed?" But that's the way the family works. I think it's the way a family *should* work. Muslims are almost never atomized people.

Consider the positive virtues of the Five Pillars of Islam:

First, you have to tell the world. Maybe just once, but you have to do it in words. No more of that "Well, I'm a private person and religion's a very personal matter, so..." You have to tell *someone*, at least *once*, where you stand in relation to religion and God. This probably does more for the teller than the hearer.

Many Westerners are resistant to talking about religion. They don't like to do it. But watch out!: your children might become Scientologists. "Mom, why did you and Dad never talk to us about religion?"

Then there is the five-times-a-day prayer. This is designed to help you remember that the credit for your life does not belong to you.

Five-times-a-day prayer is a terrific practice. I was with someone the other day who is very busy. She meditates once a week for 25 minutes. She says that that 25 minutes, in which she gets completely quiet the only time she ever does, or can, is the one really good thing she does for herself all week.

I wanted to say, Have you ever considered the Second Pillar of Islam? What if the "still small voice" could speak not once a week, but 35 times a week?

My wife was in the international airport at Nairobi a few weeks before it burned down. She happened to be near the inter-faith chapel while waiting for a flight. Suddenly it was noon, and she noticed that half the people in the transit lounge had crowded into the chapel and were saying their noonday prayers: all ages and sizes, rich and poor. My wife, who is a Christian, was moved beyond words. Time stood still for a point of reverence, and stillness.

Don't forget, ALSO, the positive power of giving alms. As non-profit organizations never tire of telling prospective donors, the big plus of giving your money away is that it makes you feel good. It is better for the giver than it is for the receiver.

In his 1936 novel *Men and Brethren* James Gould Cozzens described clerical life within the Episcopal Diocese of New York during the Great Depression. Cozzens observed that the eleemosynary programs of 'Holy Innocents Episcopal Church' on Park Avenue benefited the people of Holy Innocents more than they benefited the official recipients, who were poor people that lived four blocks to the east of Holy Innocents. It is a true cliché. Giving helps the giver.

This is also something that the near-dead can understand. He now knows, better than he knew before, that when people told him, "You can't take it with you", they were saying something true. Although he is not able to give this a lot of thought at present, he knows it's true. He has become like the character in E.E. Cummings' poem "Plato told him", who didn't disagree with war until a bullet went through his brain while he was a soldier at the front. Then he knew something, and became an instant pacifist. Everyone who dies also becomes an instant altruist.

The FOURTH pillar of fasting might have actually *saved* him, too, or at least saved him some time. Sad to say, he had put on weight. He was not "morbidly" obese, but it was going in that direction. He kept *having* to go to Bonefish Grill. He could not resist those weeknights when "Bang Bang Shrimp" were on special.

He could have benefited from a little abstinence, which is what fasting is. Observing the sacred month of Ramadan might have have saved his life, or at least prolonged it.

FINALLY, there is the pilgrimage to Mecca.

Is traveling to Mecca that much harder than flying to New Zealand to see *Lord of the Rings* sites? Is it different in essence? You are making an effort to go see a place where God once spoke to a man. You might find something out about yourself there. God might speak to you, "and for myself and mine eyes shall behold" (Job 19:27). Remember Malcolm X.

Who reading this hasn't made a pilgrimage to somewhere? My wife and I drove 2000 miles to visit a place she had lived right after college. She hadn't been back for 41 years. The trip was a pilgrimage. Was it a pilgrimage to hills and valleys? No, it was a pilgrimage to herself; and also, happily for me, to *our*selves, for I knew her then. We didn't regret a single mile of the drive, not a single 'Flying J', not a single Hampton Inn. (Well, maybe the Hampton Inn.)

If only we could all do something approaching the Five Pillars of Islam. Call it a "rule of life". See it as a loose structure of reminders and enhancements. With the exception of the first, Islam's Five Pillars of practice are, let's call them, the planting of a pennant in the ground: "Here is a way in general that I would like to live. It protects me and sustains me, and tells me I am not in charge. I hope it will lessen my stress and add to my years, of contentment and family love. It may even keep me thin."

If we could all live the Five Pillars, "What a Wonderful World It Would Be" (Sam Cooke).

Flowering Wilderness

John Galsworthy published what would be his next-to-last novel in 1932. It was called *Flowering Wilderness* and told the story of a doomed love affair between two young English people who meet after the end of World War One. The man is 'Wilfrid Desert', a poet who is brittle, brilliant, and titled. The woman is 'Dinny Cherrell', a to-the-manor-born 26-year-old who is courageous, self-sufficient, and the one to whom her entire "shabby elegant" family resort with their problems. *Flowering Wilderness* sounds old-fashioned, in time and story; but it contains a most peculiar twist.

It turns out, and here it gets uncomfortable for 21st century readers, that Wilfrid Desert, on a trip to Darfur, has embraced Islam! At the point of a gun, held by a young Muslim who had taken a religious vow and threatened to shoot Wilfrid if he did not convert, Wilfrid renounced Christianity and embraced Islam.

Back in England, nobody knows what happened; but by the time Wilfrid gets home, rumors are beginning to spread.

Galsworthy describes the great shadow that falls over the love of Dinny Cherrell for Wilfrid Desert. It is a worldly shadow, however, and not a religious one, for Wilfrid does not get shunned by his class and peers and elders because of the *religious* side of what he did in Darfur. Wilfrid gets shunned because his cowardice, if that's what it was, "let down the side". Wilfrid betrayed his "Britishness".

Galsworthy's prescient book – for why should he have mentioned Darfur, and forced conversion as the result of kidnapping, something we have become used to seeing in appalling videos of beheadings and humiliation? – broaches a subject that should almost be unmentionable in a book sympathetic to religion. That is the subject of religious fanaticism.

'Young Desert', as Wilfrid is often referred to in *Flowering Wilderness*, was forced by a young Muslim fanatic out in the middle of nowhere to choose between an inherited form of "prep-school" Christianity and the completely blunt Islam of his equally young abductor. Desert's testimony, the first Pillar of his new religion, was not completely cynical. He thought to himself, Well, I don't actually believe in an *inward* way the religion of my fathers. (Desert has the wisdom to know that the "fathers" mostly don't believe in it either.) He then reasoned, Why should I deprive this poor young man, who is so passionate about his religion, so totally convinced about it when I'm lukewarm about mine, from the satisfaction of fulfilling his vow? Being basically indifferent to the substance, why not say the words?

And he does.

When 'young Desert' is shunned back home because of his renunciation, for word gets around and nothing in the Empire was ever fully hidden, he has to pay a great price. The worst part of it is that he and his Dinny are forced to part.

Why does Islam force the issue of religion? What causes it to become violent? Why would Islam – and some forms of Islam really do – attach its great end, which is the worship of the One God by the whole world and the establishing of God's kingdom on earth through the imposition of (God's) *Sharia* Law, to the barrel of a gun? Although no nearly-dead person is particularly interested in the establishing of *any* system or set-up back there, back in the world of space and time where he used to live, he is also bound to shake his head when he sees religion used in this way.

Flowering Wilderness, which, together with its sequel *Over the River* (U.S. title: *One More River*), was one of John Galsworthy's greatest novels, displays, even though its plot unwinds in London clubs, rather than Darfur itself, and at the manor houses of the lower upper class, the power of religion to divide. Only in the Far East, to which Desert finally escapes at the end of the book, and to which this guide is about to go, does the unfortunate, misunderstood man find his peace.

Attachments, Sunni and Shiite

A problem in the legacy of organized religions occurs when "the parishioners" take the signs of religion as equal to the things signified. An attachment occurs, by which the appearance of a thing becomes the thing itself.

In Christianity the Reformation of the 16th Century was a revolution against the signs, for example the Pope and the Eucharist, in favor of the things signified: Christ Himself present with the Church and the Great Thanksgiving that lies "underneath" the Eucharist.

In the East, Buddhism was a kind of lay protest against the Brahmins' authority in setting out religious practices that didn't seem to get anywhere. Like Luther on the Spanish Steps in Rome, the Buddha said, in the midst of torturous religious exercises, 'What am I doing this for? Is this what religion really is?'

Religions require the intervention of renewers and reformers to get underneath the forms, and re-pristinate themselves. This means getting back to the original meaning of the thing. The phrase in the West was *ad fontes*: Back to the Sources. It applied to the study of Aristotle as much as to the study of the Bible.

The history of Islam raises the question of sign in relation to thing signified in ways that are as current as the morning news. Early in its development, the religion of the Prophet divided into two streams, the Sunni and the Shiite. These streams became "solid" in the lives of regions. The 'Persian' stream was Shiite and the 'Arab' stream was Sunni. Today, in the one world of internet connection, the two streams of Islam can't hide from each other. (They never really could, but now they really can't.)

The issue is attachment. The two main schools of thought in Islam are attachments to which millions of people cling as if their life depended on it. Attachment to an identity divides as surely as anything can. Under some conditions attachment can become murderous. The genocide that took place in Rwanda in 1994 came from an attachment to a tribal identity on the part of Hutus against Tutsis. Today Sunnis are bombing the life out of the Shiites. This is identity-politics carried to its logical conclusion.

The problem is attachment. Islamic sectarianism is the current expression of a religious attachment. All religions are vulnerable to this, although it is truer to say that all *ideas* are vulnerable to it. Political ideology can act the same way as religious sectarianism, for it is a religion that is not called a religion. I witnessed a professor once from one college hit a teacher from another college over the head at a football game. The professor who bonged the teacher from the opposing college was a prominent academic, a celebrity on campus. It happened in the stands, right in front of me, during a close call by the ref during overtime. Today there would be lawyers all over this.

I have even heard Theravada Buddhists call Mahayana Buddhists bad names, and that's the religion of dis-attachment. The fault is attachment wherever you find it. The Western religions have excelled in this.

Our friend overhead, who has been watching all this but is no longer in a position to take part, wants to chime in with "What fools these mortals be" ("Perfidia"). But he can barely vocalize the thought.

"And now for something completely different" (Monty Python's Flying Circus).

Organized Religions of the East

Hinduism (Vedanta)

The playwright John van Druten once delivered an address in the Vedanta Temple of Hollywood. He started his address as follows[10]:

> "There is nothing, perhaps, in the whole narrative of my personal history which would have seemed more improbable, had it been foretold to me twenty years ago, than the fact of my being where I am this morning: In a Vedanta temple in southern California, about to deliver an address on the subject of religion."

I identify with van Druten's feeling. Prior to January 2007 I would never "in the whole narrative of my personal history" have predicted that I would be about to write warmly and enthusiastically, about the world religion of Hinduism. Hinduism is also known as Vedanta, because many of its philosophical ideas come from the Vedas, or ancient Indian scriptures.

When I realized in January 2007 that I had been mistaken about who I was, and therefore about who God is, I began a new quest for understanding. This quest was bound to take me down some paths that were different from the ones in which I had been walking. Some of those paths – though not all – had proven to be royal roads to nowhere. If my previous understanding of religion was not proving completely up to the job of navigating me through the hardest time in my life, then I would have to begin looking elsewhere. The

---

10   John van Druten, "One Element" in *Vedanta for Modern Man* (New York and Scarborough, Ontario: New American Library, 1972), 405.

facts cried out for a course correction; or, at the least, for a deepening in experience of what I had been taking for granted conceptually.

On the one hand, there seemed to be elements of a "Light that Failed" (Rudyard Kipling). On the other hand, there was "the darkness that surrounds us" (Lord McCartney). I could absolutely not stay where I was, for "the night is far spent; the day is at hand." (Romans 13:12)

Who do you think you are?

Aldous Huxley's novel *Eyeless in Gaza* was the first book I read that began to shed some light. The de-construction of the hero in *Eyeless in Gaza* seemed to parallel my own. His deliverance, within a "checkerboard" narrative that corresponded, as I now saw it, to life as it is, gave me hope. There was the addition of an almost miraculous character named 'Dr. Miller'. There was a 'Dr. Miller' in my own life, too.

From Aldous Huxley I began to read the diaries and religious essays of Huxley's friend Christopher Isherwood. Isherwood's 1945 introduction to the collection of essays and talks he edited entitled *Vedanta for the Western World* made an impression on me. On the screen of PZ's panopticon, the following words from Isherwood became an instant classic[11]:

> "Reduced to its elements, Vedanta Philosophy consists
> of three propositions. First, that Man's real nature is di-
> vine. Second, that the aim of human life is to realize this

---

11   Christopher Isherwood, "Introduction", *Vedanta for the Western World*. Edited and with an Introduction by Christopher Isherwood (Hollywood: Vedanta Press, 1945), 1.

divine nature. Third, that all religions are essentially in agreement."

I did not agree, based on recent experience, that Isherwood's third proposition of Vedanta philosophy was true. And I still don't. But Isherwood endowed the first and second propositions with short, self-evident arguments. They came in the form of a dialogue[12]:

> "In my desperation, I am ready to assume, provisionally, that this Atman [i.e., God immanent, God with us], this essential nature, does exist within me, and does offer me a lasting strength, wisdom, peace, and happiness. How am I to realize this nature? How am I to enjoy it?"

> "By ceasing to be yourself."

> "What do you mean? ... How can I stop being myself? I'm Christopher Isherwood, or I'm nothing."

> "Now how do I stop being Christopher Isherwood?"

> "By ceasing to believe that you are. What is this belief? Egotism, nothing else: an egotism which is asserted and reinforced by hundreds of your daily actions. Every time you desire, or fear, or hate; every time you boast or indulge your vanity; every time you struggle to get something for yourself, you are really asserting: 'I am a separate, unique individual. I stand apart from everything else in this universe.'"

These intense and lapidary statements of Isherwood's, by which he meant to distil the core of Vedanta teaching, were convincing. They were convincing not because of their content as such, but because of the experience I was going through. I kept thinking of Bob Dylan's song, "When you gonna wake up/Strengthen the things that remain." Some

---

12   *Ibid.*, 4-5.

of Isherwood's statements seemed to express, as I thought self-evidently, "the things that remain". Especially his wry conversance with his need to stop being Christopher Isherwood matched my own disillusionment, with myself. If this was Hinduism, then Hinduism, or Vedanta, promised hope. Isherwood's words still do.

Self-doubt

In order for the insights of Vedanta to make sense, you have to start by doubting yourself. By this I mean, you have to doubt that you are a self! This is not self-evident to most people. In fact, such a doubt, when presented to you as a possible explanation of your life, runs counter to almost the whole way you think about yourself, from your first moment of consciousness as a newborn child right through to your physical death, whenever that happens.

The reason that Isherwood's words made sense to me was that I was already feeling in considerable doubt concerning who I was. I had been wrong about so much, including who my friends were, why I had taken them to be my friends, why I had delivered myself passionately into the hands of a school of thought in religion, and why I had given myself over so completely to fighting "the good fight" (I Timothy 6:12). I had been wrong about so much that I concluded I must be wrong about 'Paul Zahl'. For whatever reason, and now it seems like a mercy and a gift, I decided I had to start a whole new construction. I had to begin with the 'I' who had thought it was an 'I', and go from there.

Thus when Christopher Isherwood began to talk about stopping being 'Christopher Isherwood', that sounded right.

Can a person be reformed?

To me, the type of religion to which I had committed myself appeared to be seeing 'Paul Zahl' as a flawed person – I agreed with that – who greatly needed the help of God both to correct and improve 'Paul Zahl', and to aid 'Paul Zahl' to overcome the many chronic obstacles of his life. God was wanting to do something in me as well as do something for me.

In a moment in time, in January 2007, I saw that this scheme of religion was not entirely accurate. The 'Paul Zahl' whom I had hoped God would work in and for, had been capable of not seeing anything. He had proven himself to be blind. Therefore the problem that religion needed to solve could not be the problem of reforming a difficult character (i.e., me), but the problem of better understanding me. The problem of religion was not so much ethical, as I had thought it was – bending the 'bad' to the 'good' – but epistemological, understanding who I was. It was a problem of knowledge.

"The Antagonist"

In 1945 the historian and novelist H.G. Wells wrote a book entitled *Mind at the End of its Tether*. It is an amazing book, and was Wells' last, as it turned out. *Mind at the End of its Tether* is a hard read because, to the progressive mind of most people, the book delivers a message of excruciating hopelessness. Wells, at the end of a long creative life, had lost all hope whatsoever for the improvement and even the survival of the human race.

Wells made one very interesting choice of words, however. He gave to the over-all insolubility of human existence, both individually and collectively, a single symbolic and also proper noun. He called it "the Antagonist". He saw the impenetrability of whatever Reality that exists behind the defeating reality of all lives and life – this is not overstating Wells' thesis – as "the Antagonist". H.G. Wells was publicly and authorially giving up. He wrote that we are all, with no exceptions, up against a force, which he did not regard as personal, though it was for him universal, that cannot be defeated. It is a kind of wall somehow expressly existent to make all our dreams, visions, and hopes for human improvement impossible to fulfill. Full Stop.

The introduction of 'the Antagonist', at the end of Wells' tether of life and thought, is as insightful as anything he ever achieved. In contemporary terms, we could dub 'the Antagonist': That Which Resists Us. It is both God and not God, or rather an Unknown God that simply IS not us. It is the Other that exists because we exist. If we did not exist, then that which is Other than us would not exist. I dub the Antagonist: Resistance. The Antagonist is pure negation.

The three "religions of the book", despite their insights into many aspects of the human predicament of frustration and finality, seem to miss this negation. They set up a Story – each religion has its own specific Story – in which 'I', and we, are in perpetual struggle with that which is not 'I', and us. This is sometimes called a "conflict-structure" of thought. It is also referred to as dualism. The result of it in religious practice is struggle. And as we have read from the best-selling writer Eckhart Tolle and the once ubiquitous Barnes and Noble kiosks devoted to his books: "What you resist, persists."

As long as you are trying to face down the Antagonist, there is no pause during which you can stop and rest. "Caution: No Shoulder Ahead."

"Lay Down Your Arms", to quote an old song. But nobody ever does.

Mind at the End of its Tether upset a lot of people. H.G. Wells had a lot of loyal readers because of his early great successes, such as *The Time Machine* and *War of the the Worlds*. But his last book got people mad.

To me, the chapter on "the Antagonist" rings true. On that January Friday in 2007, I gave up, very suddenly, in relation to the Antagonist. Don't engage, I screamed to myself. Look what it got you!

People who say you can overcome the Antagonist, which is whatever form resistance takes in your life, are cheerleaders in graveyards. When I hear their voices, I want to tune in to 'Yoda', in *The Empire Strikes Back* (1980): "We look for Another."

All that is why I was open to the odd and funny Q & A that Christopher Isherwood proposed in his introduction to *Vedanta for the Western World*. I needed to start becoming 'not Paul Zahl'.

The La Verne Seminar

Religion has to be convincingly embodied. We have to see it in a credible person in order to believe it. I wish sometimes that religion could exist in the head. That is because of the kind of person I am. But it doesn't exist in the head. Even if it could, it shouldn't. Religion exists in bodily form and has to.

'Brother Bryan' was a famous preacher in Birmingham, Alabama. He died in 1941. 'Brother Bryan' was the real thing, and is memorialized in a humble and beautiful statue there. A book about him was called "Religion in Shoes". We have to see religion in shoes. The truth is, we don't see it very often.

I once asked Frank Lake, a Christian psychoanalyst in England who died in 1982, whether he had ever met a non-neurotic person. He said, "No. But I heard that there was one once."

I think another example of religion in shoes was the La Verne Seminar, which took place at La Verne College in southern California from July 7 through August 3, 1941. It was an attempt on the part of the English mystic Gerald Heard to discover whether his eclectic understanding of Eastern religion, which at that time wore the clothes, more or less, of Vedanta Hinduism, could be reconciled with and allied to the one form of Christianity that Heard believed had not been uncorrupted by falsehood and worldliness. By this one form, Heard meant the Society of Friends – the Quakers.

Heard brought some of his meditating friends from Los Angeles to La Verne College, most of them in the circle of Swami Prabhavananda at the Hollywood Vedanta Temple; and joined up with a loose core of East Coast Quakers and liberal Protestants. There were some others, too, who drifted in, almost all of them spiritual seekers who were ahead of their time.

An informal journal of the proceedings of the La Verne Seminar was kept by Christopher Isherwood, who was present for all of it, together with his friend Denny Fouts.

Later Isherwood wrote up the Seminar as fiction, in a long short story entitled "Paul".

It surprises me how little-known the La Verne Seminar is today. I think it was one of the most ambitious and visionary events in the history of religion in America during the 20th century. In my mind, the La Verne Seminar is right up there with the 1893 Parliament of World Religions in Chicago. Moreover, the La Verne Seminar took place exactly five months before the Japanese attack on Pearl Harbor. The imminence of war was on every participant's mind. This gave a seriousness to the deliberations, which bleeds through every page of Isherwood's notes. Even so, there is a puckish, non-malicious humor in the way Christopher Isherwood described the people at La Verne, which makes reading the "proceedings" a delightful experience as well as a moving one. I would like to use a few elements of Isherwood's account of La Verne as a skeleton for this consideration of Hinduism.

We should not forget, either, about our panopticon, held like binoculars but shakily, by our near-death subject as he floats in an air pocket just below the ceiling. He needs to know about Vedanta. He needs to know about who he was, down there; and who he is, up here.

"Just look over your shoulder" (Four Tops)

When Christopher Isherwood met Swami Prabhavananda in August 1939 at the Vedanta Temple in Hollywood, Isherwood received some rough instructions in meditation and a few fairly vague responses to some questions he asked. The result of this was that Christopher Isherwood began to meditate. He got rapid results.

What Vedanta gave to this chaotic but open man was a way of detaching from 'Christopher Isherwood' that opened the door to a different self, a self distinct from 'Christopher Isherwood' and existing outside him, but also somehow inside him. The possibility that such a person even existed had never occurred to him. It is the great insight of Eastern religion.

Two years later, by the time Isherwood became the scribe for the La Verne Seminar, he had begun to experience meditation as the antidote to his otherwise most alive-and-well ego, which was ordinarily charming and at times seductive. Here is a passage from Isherwood's La Verne diary dated July 16, 1941[13]:

> "Got in half an hour's meditation this morning, alone. Disturbed at first – it's amazing what a flutter just walking upstairs and talking to people can produce – but good later. Was able to pray on my knees, which I like. Unfortunately someone came in and saw me: which was exactly what my ego had wanted.

> "Voted for individual statements at discussion, because I wanted to speak my piece. Raised my voice too loud in discussion with David White. Failed in courtesy toward other speakers, and didn't listen carefully enough to their views. Result: Second watch, thirty minutes, greatly disturbed and very poor. But I did get the conception clear which Gerald often speaks of – of looking over the Ego's shoulder while it's jumping about."

This shows that one of meditation's results is the separation of the Self, the Self "looking over the Ego's (caps. *sic*) shoulder", from the self which is the ego. Right there you have a

---

13   Christopher Isherwood, *Diaries Volume One: 1939-1960*. Edited and introduced by Katherine Bucknell (London: Vintage, 1997), 174.

feature of Vedanta that is usually not a part of the "religions of the book", i.e., Judaism, Christianity, and Islam. There are mystical strands in each of those three religions that make the distinction. But it does not tend to occur within the mainstream of any of the three.

For Judaism, Christianity, and Islam, I "yam who I am" (Popeye); and God is the aid and strengthener of the "yam". Hinduism taught a new distinction to Christopher Isherwood. This distinction became everything, and it still is. I am not the self I seem, and I never was. Hinduism separates the false self that I thought I was, and that got me into this "fine mess", from the true self that is a part of God.

"... this Force"

As a result of making this first distinction, the second great wisdom of the Indian philosophy was able to make an entrance into his thinking. Because he had made a start at understanding who he was (i.e., by "looking over his shoulder"), and also who he was not (i.e., "my ego"), he was able at the same time to consider God. "Luke, the Force!"

Isherwood wrote on July 29[14]:

> "And then I thought how, if this Force, which is behind all life, could ever become the consciously controlling factor in myself – if I could ever surrender myself to it completely and fearlessly – then my life would become the most amazing adventure, every moment would be incalculably strange and new, because then everything would be possible, there would be no limitations, no habit patterns – in fact, it wouldn't be my life anymore."

---

14   *Ibid.*, 177.

Hinduism, and with it, Buddhism, is different from the three organized religions of the West. That is because Hinduism and Buddhism attempt a more radical demotion of the givenness of the self as it appears. It looks behind the ego of humans, behind the deceiving self that would gladly accept its kind of blindness. At an early period of recorded history, the Indian thinkers saw beyond the appearance of the surface self.

Christopher Isherwood, who died in 1986, was just one man, one cultivated English man, who lived most of his life, and died, in Los Angeles. But he found something out and wrote it down.

When in January 2007 I was lifted involuntarily out of myself by means of a great shock, and found myself floating on my own ceiling, I knew immediately, beyond any doubt, that there were two selves to me. There was the self who was reading some words on a piece of paper, and there was a self who was commenting – screaming, actually: "This can't be happening. Can't everybody see? This is completely absurd. It must be a dream." Two selves, two "beings", two actors, even, though it looked like one. And the true being, the New Creation "crying to be heard" (Traffic) but only just now finding his voice due to a sudden unparalleled need to find a voice, was the true one.

This was not an entirely new theme for me, for I had always stressed the intransigent "self-possession" of what the Bible called "the Old Adam". I had also been drawn to the ancient Christian theme of a New Being. At that minute, in 2007, I determined to get to know my New Being.

Vedanta, as expressed in the writing of Huxley, Heard, Isherwood, and later, van Druten, showed me the way. Funny it should come from the East, when it was blowing "in principle" from the West, too. But Christ himself had said, "The wind blows where it wills, but you do not know whence it comes or whither it goes" (John 3:8).

Buddhism

Buddhism is a practical variant of Hinduism.

It applies philosophical principles of Hinduism to the existential situation of human beings trying to live everyday lives in quiet and in peace, and offers a renewed "practice" to attain the high aims of Hinduism.

Inter-faith comparison

I don't think it is reductive to say that Buddhism is to Hinduism something like what Protestantism is to Catholicism. Parallel to Martin Luther's frustration with the religion in which he had been reared and then later trained as a monk, was the Buddha's frustration with the kinds of ascetic practice which the Brahmin teachers had taught could accomplish that detachment from the world which would issue in an end to suffering. The main difference between these two "tensions" – Protestantism as alternative to Catholicism in the 16th Century A.D., and Buddhism as alternative to Hinduism in the 6th Century B.C. – is that the teachings of the Buddha were agnostic on the question of the existence of God, and certainly on the possibility of a personal God; while the teachings of Luther laid emphasis on a person's direct relationship with God. There is a good formal comparison between Buddhism and Protestantism, and they functioned similarly in the religious history of their lands of origin.

Materially, however, the Buddha's religion was almost not a religion by the standards of the early Protestants. The Buddha believed that the religion in which he had grown up was correct in its core intention, which was to free human beings trapped on the wheel of karma from their sure return to a damnation of repeating re-births. But the Buddha did not find within the "religion of the fathers" the means or instrument by which that freedom could be achieved. He tried the Old Religion and it didn't work.

Agnostic breakthrough

Then he broke through, at a point in time and under the Bodhi Tree, to the Four Noble Truths, and consequently to the Eight-Fold Path. The Four Noble Truths are these:

1. Existence is unhappiness.

2. Unhappiness is caused by desire.

3. Desire can be eliminated.

4. It can be eliminated by following the Eight-Fold Path, which is:

Right understanding. Right intention. Right speech. Right conduct. Right livelihood. Right effort. Right awareness, or mindfulness. Right concentration.

The emphasis of his teaching was on getting where you need to go. It was directed toward releasing you from the chronic condition of believing your desires can get you to a place of satisfaction and happiness in life. You need to get a life that is not being constantly defeated by wanting things that won't satisfy you even when you get them.

Again, Buddhism was non-religious, in the sense that the Buddha took no position, or rather, actively and intentionally took no position, on the question of God. On most traditional questions of theology, the Buddha was deliberately agnostic.

Some of the Buddha's followers today, especially those who are in reaction to Christianity or cultural Christianity, sound like atheists. That is not correct. They are not being true to the Buddha's position concerning the existence of God. The Buddha was not an atheist. But he was an agnostic. We can say that the Buddha located the job of religion in the improvement of life as people actually live it. He was eager to get his students to stop living in their heads, in worlds of conceptuality. He explained that when you live in your head, you are unable to see the things that really are in front of you. You are not able to see, and experience, life as it really is.

Insight meditation

The main tool the Buddha taught his students, who were mostly monks living in the "sangha", the community of full-time practice, was meditation. The Buddha taught a form of meditation that issued in a person's dis-attachment, or at least the beginning of his or her dis-attachment, from the ego, from "baby driver". You would meditate – and can now! – and thereby become less "bogged down" by your baggage of thoughts, images, feelings, and sensations, most of which came from the past, although some were related to the future. The point of the Buddhist practice of meditation was and is for a person to live a conscious, alert life within the real and present conditions of his and her life as it actually is.

Although I held my first book on Buddhism in my hands before I could even read – it was E.A. Burtt's 1955 anthology *The Compassionate Buddha* – and although my parents, who traveled widely in the East, nick-named me after the Buddha, I did not begin to take advantage of his insights until much later, during my late 50s. At a certain point, the result of personal crisis, I became open to meditation as practiced in the "insight" or vipassana tradition. I now see meditation as the queen of all the sacraments.

Although I have partaken of six of the seven Christian sacraments, and have personally administered the seventh, which is last rites for the dying, only one, the Holy Communion, has had the same degree of impact on my life as insight meditation. When I tell Buddhist acquaintances about the effect that the practice of Buddhist meditation has had on my life, they almost seem to become embarrassed, as if to imply, "Well, we didn't intend it to go that far". I think I come across as over-enthusiastic. After all, the practice of meditation has existed in Christianity from day one. Didn't Christ spend 40 days in the desert alone before he made a single move? And didn't I see Luis Bunuel's *Simon of the Desert* back in '65? Obviously, I missed something in my own tradition.

As a latecomer to meditation, I sometimes want to say to the American Buddhists I meet, "Do you realize what you have here? Can I tell you that meditation has unlocked parts of me, big under-the-surface parts, and freed me from them

– Sayonara! "Goodnight Moon" – in ways that nothing else ever has, from talking-cure psychotherapy to drug therapy to charismatic prayers for healing-of-the-memories to sacramental confession, the laying on of hands, and unction? Do you realize what you have?"

When I say something like this to a dedicated Buddhist practitioner, they really do look at me funny. Perhaps they are so taught to separate means from ends, instruments from outcomes, that they can't or maybe don't wish to hear about results. But sometimes I feel like the Christian theologian Harvey Cox says he felt like when he first attended a guided Buddhist retreat[15]:

> "As the days went by, I found that although I was fascinated by the art history of Buddhism, it remained somewhat exotic and merely 'interesting' to me.

> The meditation, however, was something else. From the very outset, from the first hour-long sitting, I sensed that something unusual was happening to me."

Cox published those words in 1977.

Abreaction

What are the unique results I have had that could compare with Harvey Cox's "something unusual happening to me"?

To boil it down to one thing, it is the continuous experience of a sustained, intense emotional abreaction. 'Abreaction' is a term from psychoanalysis that describes the coming-to-the-surface of suppressed emotions. Something opens in you, or to you; and feelings that were buried before are

---

15 Harvey Cox, *Turning East. The Promise and Peril of the New Orientalism* (New York: Simon and Schuster, 1977), 57.

permitted to come out. The felt power of the released emotions overwhelms you.

In the past, hidden feelings would sometimes come out while I was watching a movie. An emotional movie such as *Red Beard*, by Akira Kurosawa, or *She Wore a Yellow Ribbon*, by John Ford, would work a kind of magic, and I would begin to cry. Something in the symbolism of the story would touch something inside me, and the connection would create an emotional response. (Luis Bunuel never did that to me, incidentally. Though *Belle de Jour*...)

Sometimes an old song, let's say by The Guess Who or Dionne Warwick, can do this to you. For that matter, Mahler can do it. It depends on the symbolic content of the material making its sure but unsummoned way, like a heat-seeking missile, straight to a point of vulnerability. This is because no one, no matter what the extent of your suppression in earlier life, does not have a little un-scarred tissue, a little exposed woundedness, somewhere at the surface of your being. It may even be hiding in plain sight, though it is usually screened and hidden.

There had therefore been quite a few "low-grade" examples of abreaction in my life before I started to meditate. Somehow, however, when I was guided but without psychic pressure, habitual defenses of rationalizing, conceptualizing, and categorizing began to collapse. When those defenses of mental categorizing collapsed, then feelings which had been screened for a thousand years burst through, massively and overwhelmingly. I am not overstating what happened. It was *Prometheus Unbound*.

Insight meditation accomplished in four or five "sits" something that hundreds of other approaches to the same problems had failed to do. Hundreds of other approaches!

Many Buddhist practitioners would now say, with Karen Carpenter, OK, Paul, good, but "we've only just begun". And they would be right. Now your work can begin in earnest, of living free.

But I want to reply, Can't we give some credit where credit is due? Your meditative practice, this *Wind from the East* (Jean-Luc Godard), has achieved something that armies of psychotherapists, let alone artists in plastic and image and music, have failed to achieve. Meditation is doing it!

"I'll take you there" (The Staples Singers).

At first I thought my experience of insight meditation must be unusual. I had somehow thought that meditation was supposed to make you more detached rather than more emotional, less absorbed by feelings rather than overcome by them. What did I know? I didn't even know that meditation existed in my own religious tradition. Well, I "knew" that some Christians meditated, but I had dismissed it from my mind, right back there in the Sixties, as being flakey. Wish I hadn't.

Now I observed, in halls and rooms of the Buddhist group practice – I cheated: I looked – and saw the shoulders of people in front of me shaking with feeling, yet obviously feeling better at the end. I also became convinced that the teachers up front, the experts with their gong and candles, were not fully aware of all the properties of the dharma that they were teaching. I felt like going up to some of these 'Alfred Nobels' of the inward life and trying to remind them what they were holding in their hands. But I didn't do it. I thought they would look at me funny.

Meditation gets 'Paul Zahl' out of the way. It ousts the categorizing mental self from the theater of your life.

Meditation unseats baby driver. Then reality, and I would actually like to capitalize the word, is able to get a word in. I now believe that meditation, East and West, is the queen of the world's religious sacraments.

A problem (that all religions have)

> "Not that Buddhism ignored charity. On the contrary it recommended it in the most exalted terms. And it joined example to precept. But it lacked warmth and glow. As a religious historian very justly puts it, it knew nothing of 'the complete and mysterious gift of self.'"[16]

There is a problem "on the ground" with Buddhism. It is a problem that creates a kind of cataract over the lens of the overhead panopticon which is floating loosely in the air, up by the head and eyes of our man on the ceiling. Our friend on the ceiling *needs* meditation. He needed it long before he was required to float, involuntarily by virtue of his near-death, up to the temporary home where he gets to look down on his life.

The problem I am talking about comes up in relation to all the world's organized religions. It was brought home to me when someone I knew entered the ordained ministry of my own Christian denomination after decades of practic-

---

16   Henri Bergson, *The Two Sources of Morality and Religion*, Translated by R. Ashley Audra and Cloudesley Brereton with the assistance of W. Horsfall Carter (Garden City, N.Y.: Doubleday & Company, Inc., 1935), 225.

ing law in the "real world". His work as a parish priest was difficult, and to him, with all his experience of life and law, surprisingly difficult. Someone asked him, "What exactly is the problem you are having?" He answered, "The problem is" – he paused, with diffidence – "the parishioners."

The problem of organized religions is "the parishioners".

Whenever human nature, and especially group human nature, is involved, even the best ideas get darkened. Human nature, divided between "Baby Driver" and "Someone Who's Crying to be Heard" (Traffic), between the death-grip of the ego and the birth pangs of the New Creation, takes even the very purest resources that exist for the purpose of healing and helping, and calls them in question by setting a terrible example. The problem of organized religion is the adherents of organized religion.

In the case of Buddhism, and I am speaking of convert-Buddhists because those are the Buddhists I know, the adherents are not always very kind. This is puzzling, but it is true. You hear a lot from them about "lovingkindness" (*metta*), "compassion" (*karuna*) and "generosity" (*dana*). But I don't always feel it from them. There are wonderful exceptions to this impression I have, as there are exceptions in all religions.

By comparison, many Christians I know are sentimental and foolish. They will "give away the store" to all sorts of people who take advantage of them. Christians can also burden you with a law of guilt, when it comes to being sunny and smiling, that has a strong streak of artificiality. But the Buddhists are not all that likely to be your Good Samaritan when you need one. They will say that they ought to be. Their religion teaches them to be "kind" – that's the word! They will talk about a new spirit, especially among American Buddhist young people, of engagement and active lovingkindness. But Bergson's point, from 1932, still rings true. Where is the "complete and mysterious gift of self"?

In fairness, there are many delightful and deeply interested – I mean, in people – Buddhists. But if you think you are going to get a warm personal greeting when you drive into a Buddhist retreat center, as in "How *are* you? How *good* to see you. I remember you so well from last time! How is it going in relation to that situation you talked about when you were here last time?" – if you expect something like that, you may be disappointed.

In response, a Buddhist practitioner could well say, "Paul, you are wrong on both counts. Action is more important than words, and we care by doing, not by all this hail-fellow-well-met show, which Christians like to put on as if life is a church picnic. It's easy to say you care; a lot harder, to show you care. Moreover, we don't actually believe there is a self to 'give away', as your friend Bergson says we don't do. Spiritual progress depends on a person's getting away from that kind of personalism. What Bergson calls the 'self' is an illusion, and haven't you seen that yet? Go back to high school! "

My response to that is a little sheepish. I get embarrassed:

"I have to agree with you. At least I agree mostly. Christians talk a good line, but do they follow through? Well, Dorothy Day may have, and Mother Teresa, and that fellow over there, and this lady over here, to tell you the truth. But if you are sensitive to words over actions, you've got a point. Moreover, Christians are pretty chained to an idea of 'self' that is really just the needy fooled grasping ego. Touché!" (I say.)

I still think Buddhists can do well to "up" the affect; and Christians, for their part, to tone it down.

I used to notice that cars with the bumper sticker reading, "Do random acts of kindness" were terrible in traffic. Though "they" would probably respond,

"Well, maybe so. But what about the ones that used to say, 'Honk if you love Jesus!' You call *me* baby driver?"

Yet: *The Big Red One*

Lest we forget:

Our floater, our near-death dissociated hero, is still upstairs.

He hasn't for a single second been able to forget that he is *in extremis* as a living being.

In other words, he is close to his death. It could mean extinction for him – he doesn't know – or "Something Better Beginning" (The Kinks).

What is our bug-eyed hero to make of meditation, and those two great organized religions of the East? Well, first, he now knows that he should have meditated.

Not for its own sake, maybe, but in order to have understood *in practice* that he could detach from baby driver. He didn't have to have identified, through all those years from birth to death, with that particular 'Christopher Isherwood'-like character who seemed so real to him. Meditation could have broken the stranglehold of an entirely compulsive attachment to that character. Now, death, or the imminent prospect of it, is doing this for him. Why did he have to wait until now when it would have been possible for him to "break the chain" (Fleetwood Mac) in life?

But he probably didn't meditate, and what could have been voluntary has become inescapable – appalling by virtue of its sudden unstoppable force. Death has truly come "like a thief in the night".

I think we can say that the religions of the East can explain to him what is happening to him. But it may be too late for them to do anything for him.

On the other hand, there is something that meditation couldn't do for him, even if he had done it.

Even if he had practiced meditation for a hundred years, there is one thing that meditation could not have done for him. Meditation could not have forgiven him. Or rather, meditation could not have forgiven him the one thing he was holding onto when his stroke struck.

There is almost always something. By this I mean, almost everyone – maybe *actually* everyone – has something in their life, something they have either done or something that has been done to them, that is too hot to handle.

I learned this in meditation myself. Meditation "abreacted" a thousand memories. It abreacted a thousand guilts, humiliations, and simply bad feelings from my life. But there is one that proved too hard and calcified for even meditation to deal with. It had to do with my parents and therefore went back to day one of this fakey guy who bore my name. It is built into me, as if it were a Siamese Twin. It, this one thing, could not be excised; or rather, meditation was not able to excise it. It is like a section of me, the pound of flesh in *Merchant of Venice*, that seems small to the eye but if excised the wrong way will kill you. Call it *The Big Red One*.

This is why the religions of the East, with their inspired understanding of the inherent falseness of the attaching ego, are not the entire story. As the floater, I "get it now". They were right about 'Paul Zahl'.

But I need something more. I urgently need more. I have got to get this monkey off my back.

"Dead" Religions

"Being dead, yet speaketh" (Hebrews 11:4)

When Donovan released "Atlantis" in the Spring of 1970, I completely believed him, that the present world, or whatever wisdom our present world possessed in 1970, had been derived from the Lost Continent of Atlantis, "way down below the ocean". It was a catchy song. And the *drums*, which surprised you after Donovan's soliloquy: indelible.

"The Monster That Rocked A Lost Civilization!" (*The Minotaur,* 1960)

There is a mystique about "lost" civilizations. You can walk around the ruins of them and fantasize forever. Did the people really dress like, well, *Demetrius and the Gladiators* (1954)? Or *Land of the Pharaohs*(1955)? Or for that matter, *Apocalypto* (2006)? Did they write like Virgil?

And think like Akhenaten? And rule like Montezuma? In their "lostness" to us, there is royal room for romance.

"Dead" religions, like "lost" civilizations, are just as exciting, maybe more. They have Sibyls perched on tripods over volcanos, who have strange things to tell us. They have timeless spells and mummified kings, canopic jars and the scroll by which Isis raised Osiris from the dead. They have carved solar calendars of future world destruction, together with public human sacrifice of beautiful young men. "Thousands die as millions cheer."

They have minotaurs and krakens and Charon by the Styx.

"Dead" religions are sometimes more interesting than living religions because you have to fill in the blanks yourself. Because we don't know everything about them, they can, through our imagination, become un-dead.

There is also the feeling sometimes that religions of the world's lost past are still out there, just beyond our reach but trying to get back in again, like the dinosaurs in *The Skin of Our Teeth* by Thornton Wilder. It is a well-trodden theme in supernatural fiction, the world of Arthur Machen, Algernon Blackwood, and Russell Wakefield, that the ancient gods are but a step away, silent to us, but on the threshold, "lurkers in the dark" (H.P. Lovecraft).

This chapter is a guide to three "dead" religions that were once vital and important. It looks through the panopticon of near-death at Greco-Roman religion, ancient Egyptian religion, and Aztec religion. What can we learn from religions that are not practiced now – except in the movies and on TV – but were once mainstream? Caesars, Pharaohs, and Kings believed them. Do they still have something to offer the nearly dead?

Greco-Roman Religion

"Heu nihil invitis fas quemquam fidere divis!"
"Alas! You can trust to nothing if the gods are against it!"
(Line 402, Book Two, *The Aeneid*)

In his survey of Greek religion in *The Oxford History of the Classical World*, Robert Parker notes that throughout the long run of ancient gods and goddesses, divination and sacrifice, Sibylline inspiration and underground healing, "Explicit atheism remained virtually unknown."[17] This is an astonishing observation, and incidentally underlines the uniqueness of Lucretius, in the First Century B.C., as Lucretius was probably the first atheist on record within the Classical World. Even among the later Romans, during the late Empire, there were almost no atheists. The early Christians, ironically, were *regarded* as "atheists", because they alone did not sacrifice to the gods – whoever the gods in vogue might be. Jews also refused to sacrifice to gods, but they had received a special exemption.

Ancient Greek religion was able to harmonize itself with Greek science and Greek philosophy in a way that today seems almost impossible. What was the secret of ancient Greek religion and its credibility, until, that is, its idea of the holy became superseded by Christianity in the second and third centuries?

When I say "ancient Greek religion", I also mean ancient Roman religion, because in the main outlines of it, ancient Roman religion was parallel to ancient Greek. The mythol-

---

17   Robert Parker, "Greek Religion" in *The Oxford History of the Classical World*, Edited by John Boardman, Jasper Griffin and Oswyn Murray (Oxford and New York: Oxford University Press, 1986), 273.

ogy of their gods and heroes was almost exactly the same, excepting the nomenclature, for the Greeks and Romans. Yes, the Romans were in general more practical than the Greeks, and they were certainly more wed to some absolute principles in ethics, such as absolute duty, absolute loyalty, and absolute consistency in adherence to principles, of which in general the Greeks were more skeptical. Roman religion was also a little more strictly connected with augury. (Augury was everything.)

But in its main outlines, Greco-Roman religion was one strain of worship and one stream of mythology.

Although Greek religion is more or less dead today – with thrilling exceptions in the movies and supernatural fiction – I think it still has something to tell us. Though "dead", it speaketh; and even to the nearly dead, whose fingers have now curled up from scratching for a solution to their plight.

Nature personified

The over-riding principle of Greco-Roman religion was the humility of human beings before the awesomeness of nature. That was the center of it, the key organizing principle behind it. The religion of the ancient Greeks and Romans was organized around the humility of man and woman in face of nature's massive overwhelming "face". Thus the inscrutability of the sea was personified in Poseidon (aka Neptune); the primal volatility of sex, in Aphrodite (aka Venus); the strength of women from a male perspective, in Artemis (aka Diana); the mysterious and holy element of child-birth, with also the stability of hearth and home, in Hera (aka Juno); the devastating interruption of warfare, as well as its supposed glory, in Ares (aka Mars); and the authority of fathers, in Zeus (aka Jupiter).

Ancient people personified the things they could not control, which was just about everything as they conceived it. There were forest gods, river gods, mountain gods, harvest gods, gods of sleep, gods of puberty, gods of fertility, gods of fire, gods of dreams, gods of metal, gods of earth, gods of stars, gods of the moon: no end of gods and goddesses. The principle that underlay everything was awe, and fear, in the face of all that cannot be controlled. And that covered just about every being and thing that they observed in the outer landscape. They were also aware of the capriciousness of the *inner* landscape, so they personified their inward forces, too. Existence was an amazing meek engagement with personalized otherness.

In their piety, which was the practice, in private life and public life, of their awe in face of "the other", they made sacrifices, seldom human ones though sometimes, especially in times of crisis, as in the case of Iphigenia at Aulis, even human ones. They were also champions in the reading of omens, which was called augury.

Sacrifice

First, a word concerning their sacrifices:

The Greeks sacrificed animals, usually cows and ideally bulls, with the idea that the particular god that was personified in whatever activity they were getting ready to undertake, would be pleased. That god, he or she, would, it was hoped, take the gift of the animal as proof of the good will of the sacrificers. They were intending to express their humility in the face of whatever god was personified by the activity. The result of their gift being accepted within the invisible world of the personified god, should be the god's looking favorably upon the efforts envisaged and therefore actively prospering the sacrificers.

You would sacrifice before planting a crop, or taking a trip, or buying a field, or entering on a campaign against the neighboring tribe or city-state, or getting married, or having a baby. To say it was insurance does not quite capture the feel of it. The sacrifice was a *way of asking*, as if to say, "Pretty please. And here is some sugar on top." The most common sculpted image on ancient Roman friezes is of processions of people who are about to make an animal sacrifice.

Augury

Linked to sacrifice was something somewhat more descriptive and less prescriptive. The second primary or fundamental aspect of ancient Greek and Roman religion was not about influencing events. Rather, it was about trying to understand the nature of things before you made your human intervention by means of action. This is what augury was, the divination of omens.

Augury was the science of interpreting signs of environmental life around you with a view to finding out what the relevant god's "attitude" was in relation to what you were intending. If you were to see some geese flying away from the lake at dawn, that might tell you that destiny was not on your side today: Don't do battle with the Segestans! (By contrast, it could also tell you that your enemies, the Segestans again, were about to flee your assault. The meaning of augury was not in the events themselves, but in their interpretation by a holy person.)

If you cut open a chicken and saw that the liver was larger than usual, then that might be a good omen concerning the purchase you were planning to make that day. On the other hand, it might mean that the person with whom you were doing business was asking too large a sum.

If you saw a shooting star at the rising of the moon, it might mean, "Marry that girl!" "Get me to the church on time." Or, on the contrary, the shooting star could mean that her love for you would not last, so don't go through with it.

Although this can seem like the acme of superstition to us, it was probably as good an index of probability, in the way things actually turn out in life, as any other gauge that you and I have. That goes for today, too. What's the line from Chuck Berry?: "It goes to show, you never can tell."

"Getting in Tune" (The Who)

But more than probability, divination was about something even bigger. Divination was about getting in tune with what is going on, rather than directing events yourself. Divination was an ancient form of trying to understand the environment of life. Not to control but to understand. This is a good lesson in living, because almost every time a person tries to dominate his or her fate, it ends up back-firing It's that line again: What you resist, persists.

Augury and divination were tools the Greeks and Romans used to understand where they were, and then go on from there. There was something of the *tao* to it, which is another way of saying that they were trying to "go with the flow".

Had our familiar friend on the ceiling, the near-dead hero of this book, lived his physical life a little more like the ancient Greeks and Romans, he might not have suffered the stroke that got him up there, or his "Code Red" arrest under the harsh lights of the operating room. Had our flat-lining flailer just "watched, waited and listened", he might have not done the one particular thing that wrecked his life and wrecked his health.

In general the ancient Greeks and ancient Romans were more patient than we are. Their religion made them humble. Rooster-entrails or not, it made them patient. And by the way, as the feats of their legions show us again and again, when the Romans moved, they really moved. God help you if you were a Parthian, a Briton or a Gaul when the Romans divined it was time to strike.

Ancient Egyptian Religion

"Do – not – touch that casket."
(Dr. Muller in *The Mummy* (1932) starring Boris Karloff)

In early 2011 the events of the so-called first "Arab Spring" unfolded in Egypt. The center of the Arab Spring in that country was Tahrir Square in Cairo. The Cairo Museum, as it is often called, which is the Museum of Egyptian Antiquities, is on Tahrir Square. During the famous demonstrations, which "the whole world [was] watching", as in Haskell Wexler's *Medium Cool* (1969), there was a break-in at the Cairo Museum. Several ancient artifacts were reported stolen. As a lifelong fan of the living mummies of ancient Egypt, it didn't take me long to realize who the culprits were. [Answer: The Priests of Karnak]

Immortality

The world-famous collection of mummies in the Cairo Museum tells us that the main stratum of ancient Egyptian religion concerned the question of life after death, or immortality. Everyone, even the poorest of the land, had an interest in life after death. This is why total and completely absorbing pains were taken with the bodies of the dead, and with the Royal dead most attentively. Did you know that almost all the stone monuments of ancient Egypt are mausoleums of one kind or another, or are adjacent to mausoleums?

The outstanding contribution of ancient Egyptian religion to the culture of the world was ancient Egypt's fascination with death and the after-life. The Egyptians were particularly entranced with the idea of death as journey. The soul after death was often portrayed as a person rowing or being rowed down a river on a boat.

Also, because of the annual rise and fall of the water level on the Nile, which was vital for the survival of the nation, there was an almost naturalistic belief in death, i.e., river fall, and resurrection, i.e., river rise. Add to this a very high regard for animals, an environmental humility not unlike the awe of the Greeks and the Romans, by which the lesser gods of life had the bodies of people but the heads of jackals, cats, birds, and lions; and you have the distinctive subjects of this great world religion.

As in other "dead" religions of the past, the Pharaoh, or king, was considered divine. He was a god himself, and making statues of Pharaoh with the attributes of a god was a big part of the national economy. You can say with certainty that ancient Egypt was all about religion, and its religion was all about the soul and the journey of the soul to eternal bliss.

This is an interest that Western culture has almost wholly lost. We are about holding on to physical life, about extending it, and enhancing it as we extend it. Sometimes we can be about the process of ending, or enduring the ending, of physical life, though rarely do we talk about it. Seldom, and only among kooks and purported religious fundamentalists, who are seen as reactionaries, is death discussed directly, or even mentioned.

I was at dinner with a group of retired physicians, and the wife of one of them asked me what I was doing these days. I said, "Thinking about my death and trying to prepare for it." You would have thought I had uttered an unspeakable word. Her eyes widened, she gasped, and then she put her fingers over her ears – this really happened. She said, "How can you think about a thing like that? I hate to think about things like that."

Our conversation, needless to say, changed course instantly, and we spoke about the price of summer homes in the cooler part of the state.

I love Egyptian religion! Although I know that no religion that exists in space and time can answer the question of what happens after death, "from whose bourn no traveller returns", I admire the Egyptians for thinking about it. I admire them for making it the un-denied first question of life: Why does life end, and does it? Looking, too, in the bathroom mirror at my greying hair and dreadful bushy eyebrows, I wish that I, too, could exchange my head for the head of a lion. Like the New York Public Library and the MGM roar.

Aton vs. Amon

Near the beginning of the 14th century B.C., Amenhotep IV became the Pharaoh of Egypt. The memory of his reign is swathed in romance, legend and mystery. This is because he undertook to do something that had never been done before and would never be tried again, unless you count King Edward VI of England 29 centuries later. Actually, there were a few others in between, such as King Josiah of Judah in the seventh century. But Edward VI and Amenhotep IV were truly "boy-kings". They were youthful reformers in whom the world will probably never lose interest. Amenhotep IV's reign also bears pathos, as the reforms he made were completely reversed after he died. His successors erased every single piece of physical evidence that he had ever lived. It is only because the successors of Amenhotep IV, who had been known in life as Akhenaten, did not have the technology to blow up every single block of stone on which his image or his god Aton had been carved, that we know anything about him at all.

Had the kings and priests who came after Akhenaten been able to accomplish their reactionary project – they acted just like the "Ministry of Truth" in *1984* – it would be as if he had never lived.

Akhenaten tried to do something important. Looking back on it now, I am not sure that what he thought connects with the nearly dead as much as the religion of Amon that he tried to supplant. But I am going to take the panopticon out of the hands – or are they beginning to look like claws?

– of our now jackal-headed hero, and see what we can see. I am looking for something that is practical from the reign of great Akhenaten.

"Hymn to the Sun"

> Thy dawning is beautiful in the horizon of the sky,
> O living Aton, Beginning of life.
> When thou risest in the eastern horizon
> Thou that fillest every land with thy beauty.
> Thou art beautiful, great, glittering, high above every land,
> Thy rays, they encompass the land, even all that thou has made.[18]

Akhenaten believed that there was one true and sole God, Aton, the divine Being of the Sun. Akhenaten worshipped the disc of the sun. For him, every sunrise was the renewing of the world's life and hope. As Pharaoh, Akhenaten was able to commission, although this is not exactly the right word since the worlds of art, politics, religion, and commerce all worked as one, thousands of images of the sun-disc shedding its life over the earth. Aton's kind regard for the earth was represented through hundreds of little hands generated by the sun and reaching down to us. Many images, or impresses, were also made representing Akhenaten, together with his wife Nefertiti and their children, in vertical worship of Aton, their long-fingered hands waving at the sky.

There was not much more to the new religion of Pharaoh Akhenaten than this focussed reverence of the sun. A side-effect of his nature-monotheism was that the artistic

---

18 J.H. Breasted, *The Development of Religion and Thought in Ancient Egypt* (New York: Charles Scribner's Sons, 1912), 324.

energies of the culture became directed towards "secular" paintings of birds, crocodiles, fishermen, artisans and farmers. Sacred art being reserved for one repeating image, that of the sun in relation mainly to the royal family – which represented the whole Egyptian people in the act of praise – secular art "took off", like Dutch Protestant art of the 17th century. There were "no other gods" to represent, as Akhenaten believed in none of them anymore, so artists were freed to pursue scenes of everyday life. Like everything else during Akhenaten's short reign, art took a U-turn, for a short time.

During the Christian centuries of the West, Akhenaten has been seen as the first monotheist. Sigmund Freud saw him that way, for example. There was also a sumptuous Hollywood movie made about him in 1954 that was called *The Egyptian* and based on a novel by Mika Waltari. It's a really good movie.

Akhenaten and his elegant wife, of whom a famous bust is displayed in the Egyptian Museum of Berlin, were in fact refined defeated characters. Nefertiti tried with great courage to keep the devotion to Aton going after her husband died. Their crusade has the feel of a "Prague Spring", and there was a *joie de vivre* to it that comes through in the art, secular examples of which have survived.

More recently, in our "post-Christian" age, revisers have wanted to understand Akhenaten as a negative and authoritarian "puritan", an intolerant religious systematizer. Because he believed so warmly in God, Akhenaten's views are currently in recession. He is viewed more and more today as a "fundamentalist". That cannot be true if you study the art. Akhenaten was closer to being a "flower child"! Indeed, garlands and bouquets of flowers occur in much of the work that he blessed.

What remains from the "Tell el-Amarna revolution"?

That is the current phrase for Akhenaten and Nefertiti's movement in religion. It comes from the Arab name for Akhenaten's "City of the Sun", which was called Akhetaten by the Egyptians. Akhetaten, or Amarna, was razed and abandoned after Nefertiti's "last stand" for the Sun. It is a sparse ruin today.

What remains for us from the religion of Akhenaten? What does the panopticon see?

The panopticon sees the energy and agency of *one idea*. Akhenaten and Nefertiti had one idea. They located all spiritual good in the renewal of the earth that takes place daily through the dawn of light. They placed their entire emphasis on one aspect of faith, the gift of Aton. From their point of view, they succeeded, till death did them part, in keeping the main thing the main thing. The point here is simplicity in religion.

Ancient Egyptian religion, which was anchored in the pantheon or divine family of Amon-Ra, was extremely resourceful in bringing in the animals, and the great River, and therefore the harvest. It was successful in speaking directly to the enigma of death, of which not one crumb of denial existed in ancient Egypt. The hope of immortality that was behind the burial of every mummified person was unique in the history of the world. Akhenaten tried to destroy the pre-existing pantheon in favor of one divine being. He did not regard the family of Amon-Ra as Olympian and majestic. He looked upon it, rather, as "Rocky and Bullwinkle and Friends" – a bizarre outlandish superstition that seemed to him entirely man-made. He mocked them all.

What the panopticon sees in the religion of Egypt is a positive myopia about death that could help our dying and near-dead citizens today, by preventing that denial of it which retards and intimidates us, and makes the end of life into a prolonged and horrible secret.

The panopticon also sees the concentrating power that comes from one idea. The near-dead are saying to us, "Keep it simple. What I have time for, and room for, is simple. Do like Akhenaten. Try to tell me just one thing, at most two." Walk like an Egyptian.

Aztec Religion

WE CARRY YOUR HEART IN OUR HEARTS
(Memorial inscription at Newton Park, Winter Garden, Florida)

Human sacrifice

Most of what is known about Aztec religion comes from stone sculpture and friezes on ruined buildings. Concerning the most exotic aspect of it, human sacrifice, there has been further confirmation in the skeletons of victims exhumed near the sacrificial sites. There were also eyewitnesses who gave reports to the Spanish in 1519.

An extremely vivid movie about Aztec religion was released in 2006. It was made by Mel Gibson and called *Apocalypto*. *Apocalypto* told the story of a young man, a captive, who escapes being sacrificed at the great temple and must "run through the jungle" (Creedence Clearwater Revival) to escape his merciless pursuers, and also rescue his wife and child from being drowned in a flooding cave. *Apocalypto* implied that human sacrifice was the sign of an infected culture and of a religion on the verge of being overthrown.

Another, less artistic instance of popular culture that concerns Aztec religion was an episode of the television show *Kolchak:The Night Stalker*. The episode, entitled "Legacy of Terror", aired in early 1975, and starred Erik Estrada before he became famous. "Legacy of Terror" was about a contemporary cult of Aztec priests and devotees in Chicago, which was wining and dining a handsome minor thug for a year prior to cutting out his heart inside a sports stadium in the middle of the night. What made the episode work was the trappings of 15th-century human sacrifice in the setting of 1970s Chicago. They even threw in an Aztec mummy.

Power in the blood

Aztec religion was, to put it mildly, propitiatory. It was also participatory.

The idea or mechanism of it was to transfuse the blood of a living human sacrifice into the cycle of nature and the gods, thus re-invigorating the world for the next calendar year. It was more a seasonal event – Happy Thanksgiving! – than a response to crisis, such as a drought or an epidemic, although crisis might require more occasions and more victims.

The spurting blood of the pumping heart, elevated by the priest before the people, was the essence of their new life.

And the victim, the young man whose living heart it had been, was sometimes encouraged, in a one-year period of preparation leading up to the great day, to regard himself as one with the god on earth. The victim, the Erik Estrada character in "Legacy of Terror", was both a propitiation and a part of the god. The connection was of human blood with the renewal of the earth. Just like when you get a transfusion if you need one: the earth's been watered and the fields are wet.

This is how Lloyd Fonvielle describes the Aztec cult of human sacrifice. It is from his 2012 novel *Bloodbath* (Amazon Kindle) and is part of a speech that is put in the mouth of Jack Kerouac:

> "Now most religions are obsessed with death. Your Buddhist will sit and meditate on bodily decay for days on end, but it's because he wants to move past it. Your Christian thinks Jesus killed death. For the Aztecs, though, death is like headlights bearing down on them at 60 miles per hour in a dark alley. *Huis clos*, baby. No way out. It's judging them, see, and they can't judge it back, because they're not worthy. They've got nothing to offer it back but living, beating hearts ripped out of sacrificial victims. 'Is this what you want, Mr. Death? Take it. Take two. Take a hundred.' I think it's kind of a relief when Cortes and his bully boys arrive and say, 'O. K., the jig is up. You guys are finished.' They knew it was coming, and the tension was killing them."

Massacre of the innocents

I have been to the "Tophet" in Carthage, the ancient port city of modern Tunisia. The Tophet is the site where human sacrifice was practiced, in particular, child sacrifice. It is a long stone enclosure and resembles a giant bake-oven.

Thousands of living babies were burned in the Tophet as offerings to the goddess Tanit, or 'Tanith' in English. The Tophet gives off a horrible vibe when you enter it today. You can almost smell the evil.

The only other place like the Tophet that I have ever visited was a gas chamber at Auschwitz that the Nazis did not blow up. It is where the first tests of the poison gas were administered, to Russian prisoners of war. We went there during a thunderstorm, so the chamber inside was bleeding with rivulets of water. I have not visited the sites of Aztec sacrifice.

Although Aztec religion inspired beautiful art – some of the most complex filigreed and geometric designs ever made – and although its lunar, solar and stellar calendars were precise and complex, what the world remembers are the images of young men being carved open in public, their hearts ripped out and held up high for all to see, then their dead bodies being kicked down the steep stone stairs of the temple until coming to rest on top of other bodies at the bottom. How could people do this, we ask? The answer is, most of the victims were "expendable" prisoners from raids on the enemy. The "high-value targets", to use U.S. Government language, were noble youths promised temporal delights for a year and then eternal union at the moment of death. The latter apparently welcomed their Day, although they were usually drugged at the end.

But still!

For the near-dead, the "take-away" from Aztec religion is not much. At first thought, the insatiable hunger it represents for chemical means, human blood, to renew the dying of the earth, relates to the kind of urgent preoccupation with rescue that the near-dead carries in every quivering atom of his needy self. Looking down through his panopticon of urgent need for aid and comfort, upon the ghastly drama of priest and victim that is being enacted at the summit of the Moon Pyramid of Tenochtitlan, he can feel instinctively the kind of expectation that the people feel as they watch from below. "I need a miracle every day" (The Grateful Dead).

But *this* miracle? This miracle is not about life. The killing of all these young men?: there is one report, not completely corroborated, that 80,000 captives died during a single four-day festival at the order of king and priests. There was no new life for them, save for the gilded youths.

Big Bird

There is a memorable scene of Aztec-style sacrifice in the movie *Indiana Jones and the Temple of Doom* (1984). Although the use of drugs to dull the fear of the victim is shown, the cult act of the heart being cut out of him is also shown. It is an indelible image. (Why did I ever take our children to see that movie when they were little?) I feel sure it is an image that has haunted the culture of Mexico ever since. The moment Jack Kerouac arrived in Mexico City in 1952, he said he started having dreams about Aztec sacrifice.

The near death of *our* current victim, high up on the ceiling, who can't escape watching his own heart being worked on invasively as the result of a "Code Red", has "concentrated his mind wonderfully". But not enough for him to want release by means of a flint knife and the smeared face of a man wearing a bird-costume. That would be a "textbook" instance of cutting off your heart to spite your face.

The Occult

Stigma (BBC, 1977)

The British Film Institute released in time for Christmas 2013 a box set of "Ghost Stories for Christmas", in which were collected the annual productions, mostly from the 1970s, of televised ghost stories written by Montague Rhodes (M.R.) James.

In the box set was included a disc of televised stories in the mood or interest of M.R. James, but not written by him. *Stigma*, written by Clive Exton, directed by Lawrence Gordon Clark, and starring Kate Binchy, was one of these.

I don't recommend that any reader of this book watch *Stigma*.

But it is a perfect beginning for a chapter on occult religion.

Stigma is just 32 minutes long, but in its short, devastating run manages to distill the entire substance of what occult religion is about.

Set in 1977, the year it was filmed, *Stigma* takes place at a weekend cottage in the English countryside, where a mother and her captious teenage daughter are arriving on Friday, but the father is due Saturday. When mother and daughter pull in to the cottage, two workmen are moving a giant rock in the garden, which the father of the family has paid them to move. As they grapple with the rock, which is enormous, Katherine, the mother, begins to bleed. The rock is too heavy to be moved. However, the workmen find, right under the rock as they are setting new cables around it, a heavy old knife. This has to be an Iron Age knife. The workers finally succeed in moving the rock, with earth-moving equipment, but terrible things happen to Katherine.

The story is told with almost no dialogue. A lot of time is spent with Katherine as she tries to locate the source of her bleeding. What becomes evident is that in some distant period of the past, someone was sacrificed upon the rock that is now in the garden, probably a witch; and the family has disturbed a sacred site.

Some classic themes of religion are in *Stigma*, but they are twisted. First, it is a question of human sacrifice. A person was sacrificed ritually. Second, it is a question of evil presence, dormant but alive, and ready to reach out over the centuries and grab new victims. Any victim of whatever the rite is that was once conducted on the rock will die, and they will die from loss of blood. The blood must be in some sense propitiatory. When the victim's blood is completely gone out of their body, the power that was under the rock is quieted. Third, the evil presence, or energy, is non-discriminating. It is prepared to seize any human victim that is spatially near to it. It is "no respecter of persons". All it took was moving the rock, and that was done in ignorance.

What makes *Stigma* memorable, beyond Kate Binchy's shocked performance, is the idea that a malignant force, from ancient times, can come out in the present day, when all the couple wants to do, together with their obnoxious teenage daughter, is get away for a few days and watch some television.

Trying to manage the un-manageable

There is not much primary literature concerning the occult. Or rather, there is not much *non-fiction* literature that can be consulted concerning the occult, because the whole appeal of it stems from its hiddenness. "Occult" means "hidden" in Latin, literally "covered over". Occultists will say that it is religion, authoritarian religion such as that found in Catholicism and Sunni Islam, that has suppressed legitimate written sources, most of them ancient or medieval. According to occultists, religion has blacklisted and banned evidence of "the other side". There is truth in that – 'Katherine' in *Stigma* probably wishes "religion" had done *more* in the line of suppression – but it is not true today.

In general, occultists enjoy thinking they are on the run and in danger of their lives. I think they *are* in danger, yes; but because they are trying to control something, a chimerical form of energy, that is un-controllable.

Sons of the clergy

The best way to learn about the occult, short of going on the internet and finding your own satanic mass to visit, is to read about it in the inspired stories of its fictional masters. They are M.R. James, Algernon Blackwood, Arthur Machen, and H.R. Wakefield. All of these were Englishmen and all of them were the sons of Anglican clergymen, except for Blackwood. Blackwood's father was a lay evangelist for the Sandemanians, an evangelical sect originating in the Church of Scotland (!).

There are other excellent writers of supernatural fiction, almost all of them the sons of clergymen, too. But the best examples come from James, Blackwood, Machen, and Wakefield.

A fifth supernatural writer, Howard P. Lovecraft, who was from Rhode Island, may have been the best of them all, although Lovecraft is in a class by himself. Lovecraft seems to have been cheering for "the other side". H.P. Lovecraft took the genre of occult fiction about as far as you can go. After I read his long short-story "The Mountains of Madness", I wanted to commit suicide. It was that good and that disturbing.

Fictional treatments of the occult, the best of which were all written by men who were in reaction to paternal Christianity – Wakefield was the son of the Bishop of Birmingham! – portray the occult as something that acts within certain principles, or "standard operating procedures". I would like to say what these are. Then I will ask the question, is any of it true? Is there anything objective to it? Moreover, can the occult be a support to the nearly dead, or newly dead? Could it possibly wake the dead?

"The Seventeenth Hole at Duncaster"

H.Russell Wakefield's story "The Seventeenth Hole at Duncaster" is a classic. In an ironic, detached style, Wakefield tells the story of a golf club in Norfolk that makes some adjustments in its circuit and places the seventeenth hole near a stand of trees that turns out to be the site of ancient Druidic sacrifice. Any player, male or female, who hits the ball too close to the unholy site and goes looking for it, dies of fright and shock. Blood keeps turning up, too, as in *Stigma*.

The story is one of those collisions between a pre-Christian cult and the idle pursuits of contemporary living. Modern life is speechless and unprepared before the ancient practice, which lingers impenetrably; and has to retreat, stunned, before it. Wakefield's primeval images in "The Seventeenth Hole at Duncaster" are subtle and unforgettable.

The "mechanism" behind the story is the longevity of a religion that exists to control the energy of life – Druidism in this case – and the property of that religion not "always to have mercy" (*Book of Common Prayer*), but rather to reach out and kill, draining the life of the modern living so that it can live again. Control, or the attempt to control, and blood as a vital force – comparable to breath in the Hebrew Scriptures and also in Indian meditation: these are two core principles of the occult.

"Casting the Runes"

M.R. James' short story "Casting the Runes", which was made into an excellent movie, *Curse of the Demon*, in 1957, is another classic tale of occult imagination. James was the son of an Evangelical or Low-Church vicar in the Church of England. He eventually became Provost of Eton. In "Casting the Runes" M. R. James depicts a third core theme of occult knowledge: the transfer of unseen vital energy from one person to another, as well as one man's attempt to manage the transfer for his own advantage.

Again, because the story takes place in the author's present, which is Edwardian England, ancient occult forces come out in train stations and in library reading rooms. An underlying element is the impersonality of occult energy – it doesn't make moral distinctions and "takes" whomsoever it can get – and the attraction represented to a human being of the possibility of dominating that energy. Because James was a practicing Christian, he did not wish to give his occultist villain the last word. So the manipulation involved in "casting the runes" rebounds upon the manipulator.

Personifications

Like the religion of the ancient Greeks and Romans, the occult personifies its god or gods. The most famous personification of the impersonal energy underlying everything is Satan, or the devil. Satan "wields" energy and is the manipulator in pure form. Interestingly, occultism is extremely manipulative where Christianity and Islam are not. Christianity and Islam are accepting. Islam says "Inshallah", "if God wills it"; and Christ said, "Not my will, but Thy will." Satan, on the other hand, and the occult in general, takes arms against a sea of troubles and *uses* the thing.

H.R. Wakefield, writing in 1953, observed that the kind of people he knew who became involved with Satan were bruised sophisticated souls who had come to the end of their tether and were oddly open to the "left-hand path". Wakefield described one of them in a story entitled "The Sepulchre of Jasper Sarasen"[19]:

> "Sir Reginald, like so many baffled and disillusioned persons of our time when confronted inexorably and bloodily with the human dilemma, had played – the word is apt – with the concept of diabolism."

I have met a few 'Sir Reginalds' myself – real people. They may have had trust funds in New York, and flats in London, but they looked incredibly burnt out. They are all dead now, resident on shelves in family mausoleums.

The demons and *succubi* of yore and lore are personifications of an energy that is desired for control. The energy which occultists wish to utilize for personal advantage is neutral in itself. Only when it becomes the object of manipulation – human power – does it become malignant. (Otherwise it seems to "rest in peace".) It is not the energy, personified or not, that is evil in itself. It is the attempt to dominate the energy. That becomes the un-holy element.

The occult is a kind of religion, therefore, that is not usually called a religion. It comes under the heading of power. It is about the human urge to convey to itself the possibility of effective intervention – in any sphere of life you can name.

Whether you are a student of Vedanta or a Christian nun, a Sufi teacher or a roshi Zen master, you are taught that receptive patience is the secret to living, not desire or grasping. It is ironic that the Western world now regards Christianity as the religion of control rather than freedom. It is really

---

19 "The Sepulchre of Jasper Sarasen" in *Strayers from Sheol* (Sauk City, Wisconsin: Arkham House, 1961), 148.

not that way at all. The religion of control, hiding under cover as it desires to, and wherever it may, is the occult.

Energy transfer

The most conspicuous characteristic of occult worship, by which I mean the *practice* of the occult, is the principle of energy transfer. The energy you are trying to control is dynamic and fluid. It can "jump" from one container to another. It is "shape-shifting", to use an adjective that entered the speech of the world as a result of *The X-Files*. If only a person could figure out the rules that govern the movement of this life-energy.

To do so is the concrete task of occult religion. If you read *The Screwtape Letters*, you can see that the author, C.S. Lewis, is observing a Satanic agent trying to describe those rules and understand how they work in the life of mortals.

You should almost be able to put them down in the form of propositions. This is what occultists try to do. "If I do this, then that will happen." It is supposed to be automatic, like Christian sacraments have sometimes been understood to be – *ex opere operato*. You can see why Simon the Magician in the New Testament was watching the Christians. He was trying to uncover universal laws of prestidigitation. Unfortunately for Simon, the Christians didn't have any of those laws. Their religion was not about control, but acquiescence. Remember what happened to Simon. (You can see it in the movie *The Silver Chalice* (1954). Jack Palance played Simon.)

Dying more than living

Occult religion suffers from two limitations. These two limitations are enough to disqualify the occult from competing in our race to help the dying.

There will always be an audience for occultism, even "In the Year 2525" (Zager and Evans). I personally think it looks fun, I liked *The Exorcist* when it came out in 1973, and morbid things are always interesting at first – the way an accident on the freeway is interesting. There will always be an audience for the occult.

But I'm not sure the audience includes the dying.

For one thing, occultism is more about hastening death than prolonging life. It drains your blood, literally; and "takes it out of you". That is why its practitioners are almost always described as pale and sallow, aesthenic and powdery white. I have yet to meet a practitioner of the occult who looks like George Hamilton. Though maybe in *Love at First Bite*.

The rituals of death-transfusion, through which someone *else* always gets to live a little longer, not you, "vant your blood". Poor Katherine in *Stigma*. She is a normative instance of what occultism can do for you, and in her case she doesn't even get to know what's happening. Only the grass around the big rock in the garden will get a little greener as a result of Katherine's proximity. Her blood has watered "the field".

The occult would rather have you dead than alive. There are no "Comfortable Words" (*Book of Common Prayer*) in it.

"Wishin' and hopin'" (Dusty Springfield)

Moreover, there is not an occultist on record who has ever vanquished death. Just like us, they all die. They may "get" more than we got. They may dominate other people more easily than you and I do, who have, in our human nature, let's face it, tried to do the same thing but without success. Occultists have their "Trilbys". You and I have our children, and our husbands and wives. It sure would be great if we could dominate them. Sometimes it looks like maybe we did. Our wife really does go along, *all the time*, with our ridiculous projects. One of our children really does seem to be doing what we said they should do in order to be happy, i.e., be like us.

But the truth is, none of the supposedly dominated people in our life ends up "sucking it up" forever, not one, not even the ones who look like they are. Beaten-down daughters and taken-for-granted wives have a way of leaving you, suddenly. Or turning on you with a kitchen knife.

Did you ever read the story by Roald Dahl about the domineering man whose brain was kept alive in a tank after his body died, by his long-suffering wife? Now she could take pleasure in blowing smoke rings at him – his brain, in solution, could see but couldn't talk – and "jitter-bugging" around him to loud music. Now she could drive him completely crazy after a lifetime of surface docility. The story is called "William and Mary".

No occultist has ever outlived his physical death. Some have tried and all have wished. But death is stronger than even the blood of life transfused into the earth. You can see why the Aztecs, who had an occult vision in relation to their practice of blood-sacrifice, ended up just doing it more. Way more. *Once Is Not Enough* (Jacqueline Susann). It really was reported to the Spanish, by more than one witness, that during the four-day festival in 1487 to dedicate a new temple, 80,000 people had their hearts torn out by the priests. I don't believe this number, but there must have been a lot to get the story going.

What our upstairs friend, of whom we have to remain mindful because he stands for all of us in our hour of dying, requires from a religion, is relief from his pain. That pain is in relation to the suffering and also the blame of his past life. He is like a balloon tied by a long ribbon to an anchor. He won't sprout any wings as long as he is tethered to its weight. Occult religion is too selfish to care about him – "Who gives a flying f___ what the Church of Scotland thinks?"

Occultists have not dis-attached from their own lives. They are working very hard for themselves. They want to live on, but in the form of "Paul Zahl", or for that matter, "Anton LaVey". This plan has never yet worked.

Religions That Are Not Called Religions

"Everything is a drug. Family, art, causes, new shoes…
We're all just tweaking our chem to avoid the void."

-Joss Whedon[20]

There is a triad of human desire that usually boils down to sex; things, or the acquisition of things; and fame, or celebrity. These three things are what most people, at least when you strip them down to basics, believe can give them happiness. Therefore they strive to get them.

Each of the three things, sex, things, and fame, is engrossing, sometimes completely engrossing. Each of them also carries a kind of obsessional possibility within itself, by which enough is never enough. You end up "feeding the beast", like a heroine habit. The thing becomes what you live for.

---

20 Joss Whedon. "Everything is a drug. Family, art, causes, new shoes… We're all just tweaking our chem to avoid the void." 27 June 2013, 5:58 p.m. Tweet.

The trinity of desire, which has been pointed out by poets and philosophers since words began, is easy to de-construct if you believe in religion as a constant human drive. That is because sex, things, and celebrity function the way religions function. In other words, we worship them! People, especially men, worship sex. (Everybody worships love.) People worship things, or having things. People can't get enough attention, i.e., fame, which is the collective form of attention, if and when they ever get it at all.

Sex is easy to turn into something to worship. Sex is worshipful.

Things are easy to worship, especially if they are beautiful. As Joss Whedon says, "new shoes" can be a drug if we don't watch out.

Fame *is* a drug. Have you ever known anyone "famous", any celebrity, who did not want to stay famous? Case in point: *Sunset Boulevard* (1950).

More than just formal

I am saying that religion is more than just formal religion. It is more than Vedanta and Islam, more than moon pyramids and forest nymphs, more than *succubi* and Lorelei. It is more than *bhakti*, *prana* and the Immaculate Conception. Religion is whatever is worshipped. Whatever you worship is your religion. "Drink to me only with thine eyes, and I will drink with mine" (Ben Jonson). "You're my everything, you're my everything, you're my everything, you're my everything" (Temptations).

This chapter considers six "religions", as I call them, that are not usually called religions. It widens the field of vision.

I hope you won't resent it. You may say, "Well, that's confusing apples with oranges. How can he say that wanting to have sex is a religion. It is not a religion. It's not about 'God'. Religions are about a 'supreme being' that religious people call God. That is not the same thing as wanting a new pair of shoes. Or wanting the person who's trying them on!"

I am saying that it is. Not all the time. But sometimes. Fairly often, even. Religion can be the same thing as wanting a new pair of shoes. The reason I am saying this is that buying a new pair of shoes, if you think it can supply happiness – and it can, by the way, for a pretty long time – is often based on the unsaid idea that a thing can fill the need we seem to have to fill up something in us. I don't know exactly what it is that's needing to be filled up. I never bought the idea that everyone has a "God-shaped hole" inside them. The idea I do buy is that everybody *wants*. Something. As the Buddha said in the second of the Four Noble Truths:

Unhappiness is caused by desire.

Do you remember a movie called *The Hunger* that starred Catherine Deneuve and David Bowie? It was about vampires in New York, in the Eighties. I didn't think it was very good, but the title: yes!

For the characters in that movie, the hunger was for literal blood. It superseded all other hungers. Even a love that reached down from ancient Egypt – we got to see Catherine Deneuve dressed like Nefertiti – was superseded by her habit-hunger for new blood now. I would say that her hunger was religious because its object transcended all others in importance.

I am not saying that wanting a new pair of shoes is religious in itself. But when wanting a new pair of shoes is *the thing*, like Imelda Marcos supposedly, then it is acting like a religion.

Maybe this chapter is about things that are not called religions but act like religions.

Let's talk about sex.

Sex

Sex is a worship-inspiring drive in humans, and especially in men, that *cannot be over-estimated* in its power. It is *impossible to exaggerate* the power of sex. It cannot be done and shouldn't be done. We have to stick to the truth when it comes to sex.

This book needs to go on record and say what it means. The physical pleasure of having an orgasm is, at least for a man, for whom having an orgasm is easy, the closest thing to transcendence that most people are ever going to get. "Nobody gets too much heaven no more" (The Bee Gees).

Sex is heaven.

I was with a friend once, visiting *his* friend, a college classmate, in London. The college classmate had suddenly become successful in business. He was enjoying the kind of expensive London life-style that quite a few people are certain they want. It is usually short-lived. This is because it is supremely expensive to maintain unless you are a billionaire.

In any event, the man we were visiting had just gotten married. My friend and I came with an advance reputation for being newly religious, and the classmate-friend was a little bemused by what he had heard about us.

One night we got back to the house around 11:30 and he met us downstairs in his bathrobe. He had just had sex with his wife, and she was upstairs smoking a cigarette. He was also a little drunk. He said to us, slightly slurred but with a big grin on his face, "The only religious experience I have ever had is having sex with my wife. That's my religion. See you in the morning."

I never forgot that. We were being told something, something I already knew was true but had never heard someone say in person. Part of me – although the man's tone was sanctimonious, especially as both his visitors had no dates and were an ocean away from their girlfriends – wanted to shake his hand. I wanted to say, "Thank you for telling the truth. Nobody tells the truth about sex." But another part of me wanted to say, "But wait. Is that all there is?"

Closest thing to self-transcendence

Sexual intercourse is the closest thing to self-transcendence that most of us will ever get. An orgasm is the most specifically focussed pleasure it is possible to have, although heroine addicts say the same thing about their first experience with heroine. Maybe in a war for some cause in which you believe, you can also get close to self-transcendence. The experience of combat has a long history of disillusioning the most idealistic warriors.

I put it out, in this guide to world religion, that sex is a world-wide religion that is not called a religion. It is second only to power in its undying attraction.

What is it about the sexual act that has caused it to be worthy of the most intense worship and concentration throughout the whole history of the world?

There are several theories. Some of them use words like the "imperative" of procreation or the "adaptation" of evolution. Certainly the requirement that we reproduce is going to put the means of reproduction at the center of life. But I am not a biologist. What I think I know, and what I believe most people know, just from living, is that the drive is in-built. It suffers less diminution as our bodies age, especially in the libido of men – though it suffers some diminution – than almost any other function. Men and women feel this drive in different ways, and the body-clocks we have seem to run differently between the sexes. But of the three main drives, including all the other religions that are not called religions – the religion of power being the strongest of them all – sex is the next to last to go when you lay dying. Power is the last.

Achilles Heel

Because sex is almost synonymous with the baby driver that runs the world, it is something with which religion deals, though in many different forms. Temple prostitution was a real activity in Greco-Roman religion. It took place at many sacred sites, "Town and Country". Occult religion has also always specialized in sex, specifically public sex. Some forms of Hinduism offer sexual release, and also sexual control, in their worship. Judaism takes sex very seriously, both in limiting it and also celebrating it once you limit it. Islam hides sex, but enjoins plural wives.

The organized religion which has had the least success in dealing with sex is Christianity. Christianity's failure in this area is massive, and has contributed to the recession of Christianity in Western countries. Of all the world's organized religions, Christianity has gotten the worst reputation for dealing with sex.

This is unfair, incidentally, as some forms of Judaism are no less stringent than Christianity; and Islam is more puritanical than Christianity is in most of its forms. It is unfair that Christianity is the main object of objection today due to its received misgivings about sex.

On the other hand, it's true! Christianity feared the body early on. It feared sex and the volatility of sex, and did injustice to its original confidence in divine grace when it started "laying down the law". If there hadn't been fear of the body and the body's ecstatic feelings, Christianity would not have become, as a whole – and it happened quickly – suspicious of sex.

Moreover, Jesus was not married, nor was St. Paul. There was always the idea that it was better, or more personally consecrated, to not be having sex than to be having sex, even if it was with your life-long wife or husband. A celibate monk or priest was better than a married lay person.

The history of Christianity is sour on this essential aspect of human experience. If you try to control it or suppress it or smear it, you will get back the most powerful reaction that it is humanly possible to get. Such a reaction is what the religion of Jesus is up against today.

Ironically, and again unfairly, the religion of Jesus himself majored on acceptance and inclusion. It majored on the acceptance and inclusion of sexual actings-out as much as anything else. The fact that women in that culture went around with Christ almost as much as men did, and that sexual sin was specifically forgiven and not held against the doer on several occasions in the Gospels: this means that Christ was ahead of his time and culture in the understanding he had of sexual life.

It may be too late to re-habilitate the religion of Christ in relation to sex, sex being the most powerful motivator in the world. Personally, I wish Christ had been married. (The Buddha never married after his enlightenment. Before enlightenment he *had* been married, but after that he said goodbye to sex.)

Jesus himself, the small-town Jewish carpenter who had an easy way with people, was not conflicted about sex. He treated everybody the same, and went out of his way to shield sexual offenders.

If we stick with the man himself, there is no problem.

Do the near-dead have sexual feelings?

A man who was in late middle-age once told me that he was relieved he no longer had strong sexual feelings. He was beginning to feel untroubled by temptations that had once been unwelcome to him in the past.

Later on I found out that the man was not telling the whole truth. Whatever freedom from his "baser instincts" that he had been talking about when he talked to me, the temptations had apparently flared up again. Things I saw indicated that he was being plagued again, by himself.

What this divided man was trying to say, and sincerely wanting to feel, was that the "spur" of sexual lust is a troubling thing. It has big 'Danger' signs posted all around it. Sometimes it would be better not to have it "ringing your bell" at all. Some old men do report that they feel "freed" from feelings that once filled them with temptation. Those temptations, if acted upon, would break their deepest promises and hurt the ones they really love. Socrates said that late in the game he stopped being troubled by lust.

When I saw a newspaper photograph of an extremely ancient American author holding a newborn baby whom he had fathered, I saw a truth that I had not seen earlier. The sexual possibility in many men stays green right up to the moment they die. I knew Victor Hugo had stated this in his extreme old age, as well as Leo Tolstoy. But it took that picture of a famous American Methuselah cradling his infant child to prove it to me.

Do the near-dead desire sex?

Yes and no. They do and they don't. The drive is so intrinsic that even in hospitals, old men get excited by their nurses. I've known widowers of 90 who married their nurses who were 40 or even 50 years younger than themselves. Age is not a barrier to having the desire.

On the other hand, you can't do it when you're having a heart attack. Or rather, you can't sustain it then, as there are many men who have died of heart failure during intercourse. A famous American politician did.

You can't do it after having a stroke either, although some men do. Advanced prostate cancer also makes it impossible to have sex, though not always.

Even as I write this, I am changing my mind. The near-dead *can* have sex. It is too much a part of their physical self to be shut down by anything short of death itself. We do know that dead people can't have sex.

No wonder that given the in-built strength of it, sex can become a person's religion. As my friend's crowing classmate said that night in London, sex is a religious experience. It expels you from yourself, for an instant. But that instant!

Is there sex after death?

Is there sex after death? Jesus thought not. Naturally I hope there is. To our man on the ceiling, we have to stay agnostic about it. What the man on the ceiling would tell us now is probably this:

"I don't need to know right now about sex. Maybe later. If there is a later. Just keep me breathing, OK? And tell me who I am when I stop breathing, too, OK?"

Things

It always seemed obvious to me that possessions can't satisfy a person.

Even a Stradivarius or a signed Kerouac – which I could have acquired for $46,000 in Boston recently – or a signed Galsworthy theater program, which I just *missed* acquiring at the Strand Bookstore in New York. (The irony is that I did pick up a signed Philip Wylie on that visit. But it was his worst book, *The Innocent Ambassadors*!)

It always seemed obvious to me that a desired thing, as soon as you actually had it, led to your wanting something else.

But this is not as obvious to people as I used to think. If you think most people "get" the emptiness of things, you will be disappointed. Possessions are a form of hypnosis. The belief that the acquisition of them will satisfy is deep inside us. There is an uncomfortable song in *Promises, Promises*, the musical play by Burt Bacharach and Hal David, when the head of personnel, 'J.D. Sheldrake', sings about "wanting things". His want of things extends to 'Miss Fran Kubelik'.

Mr. Sheldrake doesn't understand himself. Why, he laments to himself, does he want things so much – and to him people have become like things – when he already has so much? Even this "successful" character, who has come to an extreme end of his hunger for things, cannot begin to rescue himself from the web he has spun. Mr. Sheldrake is a lost soul. Fred MacMurray played him in the movies.

I used to think on Sunday mornings that if I just got up there and said the words, "Lay not up for yourselves treasures on earth, where moth and rust doth corrupt and where thieves break through and steal; but lay up for yourselves treasures in heaven, where neither moth nor rust doth corrupt and where thieves do not break through and steal", everybody would nod their heads and say "Yes!". Then the people would act on it. A few did.

William Inge asked to play "Reverend Whitman" in the movie he wrote called *Splendor in the Grass*. Inge composed a short sermon for the movie, and delivered it himself. It consisted of one thing, the minister's recitation of those old King James words about not laying up treasures on earth.

William Inge's sermon as the Episcopal rector in the small town of *Splendor in the Grass* is terse, and stands out in the middle of a tempestuous story.

Even in the days of the first Christians, when everybody pooled their possessions after Christ's command, there were a few who wouldn't. Interestingly enough, they died, suddenly. The New Testament, in reporting their deaths, is expressing something true to life and not judgmental. Stingy people are possessed by fear, and fear will cut you down whether you know it or not.

"Just a little more"

The reason that wanting things falls down over time is that you always want more of them. John D. Rockefeller had been a member long ago of the parish my wife and I served for six years in Westchester County outside New York. He eventually built his "own" church a few miles away. John D. Rockefeller's estate, 'Pocantico Hills', abutted our rectory on Route 9, and in the 1960s it was the site of innumerable cigarette ads that were shot there. "You can take Salem out of the country, but you can't take the country out of Salem." I wonder when and where old Mr. Rockefeller posed and answered his famous question: "How much is enough money?" His answer was, "Just a little more."

Tomb of Ligeia (x 8)

You always want something more.

I am a bush-league hoarder like everybody else.

Can I ever own enough Edgar Allan Poe movies directed by Roger Corman?

Well, there are the old VHS versions (Pan and Scan), the newer DVDs (Letterbox); and now the BluRay versions are coming out, in HD. Can I withstand the temptation to buy another copy of *Tomb of Ligeia*? The short answer is no. Absolutely not! I cannot resist the temptation of owning a slightly better copy of *Tomb of Ligeia.* (It never looked that good in the theater, by the way, the eight times I saw it.)

These things just add up and grow, and end up in big boxes in storage. (Though not the Cormans. But you know what I mean.)

The answer to whether Mr. J. D. Sheldrake's conflicted, perpetual "wanting things" will ever be satisfied is no. It will never be satisfied. Mr. Sheldrake will continue to live as if wanting things is the most important thing in his life. It is a "Chain of Fools" (Aretha Franklin), and he is one of the links in a very long chain. Aldous Huxley said of the repetition compulsion that stamps human desire, that it makes life a succession of "one damn thing after another, until you get to the last damn thing, and then there's nothing more."

Wanting things gets obsessional. Whether it's shoes at DSW or men ("It's Raining Men" – The Weather Girls), new formats of *I Married a Monster from Outer Space* or another cat in the house – there is no end to it. "Shop till you drop." Drop dead.

Little tabs of chocolate

When it comes to the man on the ceiling, material possessions have lost their specialness. He can't hold onto them, for one thing. Even his Montblanc pen won't stay in his breast pocket, not to mention his comb and chapstick. And if he's his wife, his purse is floating all over the place, and there's gum and little tabs of chocolate and credit cards and kleenex. Things have lost out completely, as a lasting good, so far as our floater is concerned.

We don't need to worry about disillusioning him about possessions. His near-death accomplished that in seconds.

Fame

In 1984 an English singer named Nik Kershaw released a song called "Wouldn't It Be Good". It became a hit in England and America. The MTV video of "Wouldn't It Be Good" was haunting. As a result of it, we expected great things from this talented man.

Fifteen years later, in 1999, Nik Kershaw released an album called "Fifteen Minutes". There he mused about the "15 minutes" of fame that he had had – though it was more like 60 weeks. To Nik Kershaw, judging from his song, it felt like 15 minutes. "Fifteen Minutes" the album was one of the first CDs I ever had stolen out of my car. It happened in 1999 in the church parking lot, and was one of ten CDs I had left on the back seat. I had about 15 minutes with "Fifteen Minutes", and think about this a lot.

Celebrity, traditionally called fame, is a passing thing.

It is extremely exciting and a big turn-on, like a drug, we are told. Think of "Stryper" or even that German band "The Scorpions". Remember Klaus Meine and Matthias Jabs? I wonder what they are thinking now. Fame is a candle with a short wick.

Yet people pursue fame with intense concentration. Once they get it, and it can come to anyone for almost any reason at any time, it feels very good. But unless you're extremely agile and can think ahead concerning how to "re-invent" yourself, fame never lasts. By definition it never lasts. "When you're hot, you're hot. When you're not, you're not."

El Cid

I saw a famous rock group in concert a couple years ago. They were on a "reunion tour". Their songs are timeless and have never been stolen out of my car. But to see them now! – and I'm all over them in principle.

They were like zombies on stage that night. I thought I was watching *El Cid*, the 1961 "spectacular" with Charlton Heston. You know, the scene when 'El Cid' has died but they put his body on a horse and brace it so the enemy will think 'El Cid' has come to life again. That's what this rock 'n roll reunion looked like: 'El Cid'-like bodies seeming to play musical instruments but the real players were standing behind them. One of the original guitarists had three players covering his part.

Fame is something you cannot re-capture. Sometimes famous people are forgotten but later "come back" due to something completely different they have done. Comebacks are a surprise to the people who make comebacks. Who would have thought that Algernon Blackwood, the writer of supernatural horror, would later "come back" as a writer of popular books for children; and then, near the end of his life, come back again as a radio personality on the BBC?

Or 'Lord Buckley', the 'Beat' comedian of the 1950s. Did people in the 1950s know that 'Lord Buckley' had once been an emcee for dance marathons during the Great Depression? He had emceed the kind of contest that was dramatized in the movie *They Shoot Horses, Don't They?* (1969). That was at least 20 years before Richard Buckley was on *The Groucho Marx Show*.

"Fame (I'm gonna live forever)" (Irene Cara)

Fame is chimerical, unpredictable, thrilling, and totally disheartening in the loss of it. Our near-dead subject on the ceiling is not, to be honest, thinking about fame, even if he may have had some once. It was nice while it lasted, but fame is one thing you definitely can't take with you.

Family and Children

People sometimes make their family, and especially their children, into a religion. They can easily turn into parents who worship their children.

We know that men worship women, because women give them an ecstatic moment of physical pleasure. The roles can be reversed, to be sure; and sexual worship applies to same-sex relations, too. Sex seems divine, although it is mostly passé to the near-dead. It is completely passé to the dead.

Children to gods

To their parents, children can turn into gods. This is bad for the children.

It is bad for the children because no human being can sustain being worshipped. Not one. When you are put on a pedestal by someone, you end up having to work to stay there. No one can do this for very long. Or rather, no one can do it for long without starting to lie and put up a false front.

When children become gods and parents, their priests, you have the set-up to a major reaction, and a major desertion. I have this seen this happen in front of me so many times that you just can't say it enough. No one believes you when you say it, however – at least not the parents, who are the high priests of Kaylee and Justin, and Josh and Caitlin.

The religion of one's children was brought home to me very soon after I was ordained. I was visiting a family in Queens, members of the parish where I was a minister, and they began to tell me about their grown daughter. She must have been about 40 then. They hadn't talked to their daughter for 10 years. They asked me to come upstairs with them and visit their daughter's room, the room in which she had been a little girl and then a teenager. Not a single item, pillow, picture or lamp had been touched since their daughter left. The room was a shrine. I thought of Francois Truffaut's movie *The Green Room* (1978). I realized I was standing on "ground zero" of a suffering worldwide fraternity, the temple of the child as God.

"Possession Obsession" (Hall & Oates)

If it seems to "come with the territory" for a man to worship his job, or at least put his emotional eggs in that basket; it seems to come with the territory for a mother to worship her children, or at least come close to doing so. It is the most "natural" thing in the world. In fact, you can fall in love with your children, especially when they are small, in exactly one beat of your heart. Many times I have heard young mothers say, "I didn't know it was possible to love someone this much."

Such talk may be natural, but it is also dangerous. It is dangerous to the child, who really doesn't wish to be loved that much, that way. It is a burden if a child matters *that much*, and in *that way*, to her or his parents. It sets up an ancient inherited curse that is the way of all flesh, and is expressed to its logical conclusion in the ancient Greek myth of Oedipus.

When parents talk thus, rhapsodically, about their children, I want to warn them, saying, "Yes, I know that's how you feel. Most parents do. But there's going to come a point when you'll have to listen to Sting: 'If you love someone, set them free'. And that point is going to come as sure as the turning of the earth. Get ready."

I am perfectly aware that you can't warn parents about the separation to come. They want to shut their ears. "That Paul Zahl again! How did we get such a de*press*ing rector?"

But if you are a parent and don't understand about the need your child was born with, to separate and become their own person, then the separation will end up being violent. I don't mean violent physically, but it will involve a tearing and a ripping; and no phone calls, like my one-time parishioners in Queens, for ten years.

There is a scene in William Inge's play *Picnic*, which was made into a very good movie in 1955, in which a young woman decides she has to break away from her mother, who is possessive, and follow her heart. As it was filmed by director Joshua Logan, the daughter, who is played by Kim Novak, has to break away physically from her mother's embrace. You can hear the ripping.

But you can't hear it up here on the ceiling

I don't think the nearly dead worship their children, at least not any longer. They would certainly like to *see* their children at the end. They could certainly use the *aid* of their children at the end. But once they begin to fade up, as our near-dead personage has begun to do, there is not much help they can get from the gods they left behind them. Their faces start to fade, almost like the Cheshire Cat. You can't take your child with you, and you shouldn't want to.

Fissures and lies

The big reason to not turn your family, and especially your children, into a religion is that it damages them. Nobody can withstand being worshipped. This is obvious from marriage. If your husband adores you – "You're my everything, you're my everything, you're my everything, you're my everything" (Temptations again) – you won't be able to be very honest with him, at least about your negative feelings. If your wife thinks you are the Rock of Gibraltar, you are not going to want to let her know when you're feeling cracks and fissures in your foundations. She will lie, and you will lie.

Family and children as your religion is like the Wizard of Oz. Life exposes the wires and the mirrors. Better to let the ones you truly love stay human, like you.

Ideology

It constantly amazes me how closely people can get attached to ideas. Ideas can make people hate. They can make people kill, in groups. They can make people give *The Best Years of Our Lives* (1946) to projects that override personal relationships, only to fail and disappoint over time. They can make people rationalize actions that have little of love in them and lots of control.

I worked in a setting once where a senior colleague described himself as a "Yellow Dog Democrat". By this he meant that he was so committed to the ideology of the Democratic Party that he would vote for a "yellow dog" if the yellow dog were running on the Democratic ticket. I got used to him reminding me, weekly, that he was a Yellow Dog Democrat. He also said that I should consider him an "ideological liberal" on any subject that might ever come up. He was, in short, as tight as a drum!

What are we talking about when we talk about ideology? Why is ideology a religion that is not called a religion?

Tight fit

Ideology refers to concepts and judgments that exist in your head and are imported into the sphere of action for the purpose of making outward reality correspond to the picture you have in your mind. Ideology is when you try to bend external circumstances to fit an idea you have, according to which those external circumstances should be able to "set", like a jello or pudding, and turn out the way you want them to be from your mind. Ideology is mental and categorical, and therefore different from that which is concrete and individual.

We all have ideas, sometimes very strong ideas, about the way people should act or the way society should behave. For example, everyone ought to share what they have. Or, men ought to think like women. Or, women ought to know what men are thinking without having to be told – like ESP. Or, people should want to clean up their neighborhoods. Or, people shouldn't smoke because smoking causes cancer. Or, college students shouldn't get drunk because then they do and say things that drunk people do and say.

The idea is basically that you should be like me. I have an "idea" of myself that is good and right. You should be like me, therefore. 'They' should be like 'us'. Why in the name of social progress can't New Yorkers stop drinking big sugary soft drinks? Let's put up 100 signs – no, 100,000 – to make sure nobody does what they shouldn't do. It's for their own good.

Soviet geneticists tried to change the laws of agriculture during the 1930s, in order to fit some theories that had been developed to go along with ideological socialism. The trouble was, the seeds and crops would not cooperate. Millions of people are supposed to have starved to death as a result.

Ideology can affect families, as in "Why can't you be the kind of son Dad has an idea of in his head?" "When will you begin acting like Hailey over there, who is Mother's idea of what you should be like? *When*, I ask you?"

Twice in my life I have known girls who were given a boy's name because their father wanted a boy. He had an idea of what he wanted, and the idea, which was in conflict with the reality, resulted in his daughter getting a risible name. She never forgave her father, by the way. Every time she had to explain to someone else about her name, which was five times a day, salt was rubbed in the wound.

"Socialist Realism"

Ideology also affects groups. It has a chronic tendency to subordinate individuals to groups, and personal life to group life. Recently I was in a museum in China where there was an exhibition of giant-sized paintings in the style called "Socialist Realism". The paintings depict events in the history of the Chinese Communist Party during the twentieth century. They are humanist masterpieces, with happy groups of diverse people gathered around proud magnanimous leaders.

However, the fact that outside the canvas – just beyond the borders of what the artist has painted – were, in the real history of the events themselves, piles of corpses, and crowds of cowed people: that wasn't shown in any of the pictures. The *idea* of the paintings overwhelmed the facts they were supposed to represent. How would a museum-goer like me know? Fortunately – I think – I was with people who knew what actually happened. If only the facts could match the happy, noble faces.

Ideology was religion to the National Socialists. It was religion for the Soviet Army's "commissars" in the Great Patriotic War. Those people were willing to die for their ideas. You can tell when ideology is in the system when the ideologues themselves begin to hide their heroes' failures. If the idea is correct, then how can our exponents of them possibly fail? It must be the other side who are lying. We won't be let down.

Ideology can sound like a religion if you are on the right and a religion if you are on the left. Wasn't there a book published in 1949 entitled *The God That Failed?* It was a series of devastating essays by writers who had become disillusioned with Communism.

No traction

Ideology provides no traction to a dying man. It gives him no rope up, no bannister down, nothing, not a single damn thing that could actually stabilize him as he's floating in the air. Moreover, he can barely put two words together in his throat. His hearing is terrible because of the whoosh. Now you want him to sign *The Communist Manifesto?*

Power

Together with sex, power is the primeval religion. It is probably the last of the religions that are not called religions to "go". You can be a hundred years old and still get a charge out of having power and using it.

Case study

The "Edward Snowden Affair" of 2013 was a case study in power. Whatever Edward Snowden actually did or didn't do in relation to the law, and whether he should be considered a whistle-blower or a traitor: those are interesting questions. But the most interesting aspect of the case was the way that journalists and media figures lined up in large numbers to defend the United States Government's actions in creating a level of surveillance here and overseas that was without precedent in American history, and ran counter to the spirit and the letter of the Constitution. The most interesting aspect of the "Edward Snowden Affair" was the way that ideologically "liberal" journalists jumped to the defense of extremely "illiberal" programs conducted by the U.S. Government.

On the face of it – and there were too many examples of it not to be noticed – these writers and journalists who rounded on Edward Snowden were going against their ideology, which supposedly had to do with values such as personal freedom, the right to privacy, historic skepticism in the face of "Establishment" claims, and theoretical sympathy, in principle, with independent thinkers. Had not they, or their ideological predecessors, been almost all on the side of Daniel Ellsberg during the early 1970s?

Power over ideology

What was the cause of this apparent inconsistency?

The solution could be that power is the most tensile and persistent of the religions that are not called religions. When you have power, or are standing in proximity to power, it has a strong, almost physical attraction. You want to stay near it, and also have some of it yourself.

A few times in my life I have been close to power. Not Presidential power. Not political power or even municipal power, though I've known a mayor or two. But, contradiction that it sadly is, church power. I have found myself close to members of the hierarchy, the people who, when they decide they like you, things begin to happen for you. In myself I have felt the attraction to people who have power, and especially if they are in the newspapers a lot. I understand about Bebe Rebozo.

Extreme reluctance

Power, when people really have it, is only relinquished with reluctance. I would say, with extreme reluctance. Twice I have been with people who had been powerful in politics but had finished their terms of office. When I was with them person-to-person, it was just *after* they had left office. When they came to the Big City as private citizens, they no longer got the penthouse suite at the Plaza. They were lucky to to get the "maid's room" on the second floor. This really happened. My wife and I had to sit with a man whose life, from his point of view, had become one long humiliation. That was the cost, as he saw it, with bitterness, of leaving a post that had carried authority and prestige.

We think of a President, let's say, as being an "ideological liberal" on many issues. But we forget about the power side of it, and what politics is all about. We suddenly see a leader who seems more right wing than the right wingers when it comes to foreign policy and military affairs. It's fine to talk about "group incarceration" in prisons here at home, but "let's lock the door and throw away the key now" (Jay and the Americans) when it comes to Guantanamo and foreign detainees.

Power trumps ideology and is superior to it. Power gives more pleasure to the one that has power than being right does.

I sometimes wonder what my old colleague the "Yellow Dog Democrat" thinks about drones and Gitmo. I wonder whether, in *his* case, ideology has trumped power.

End in itself

The point of this is not politics. There are sincere differences of opinion concerning drones and Yemen and Syria, or the best balance between personal freedom and national security. But power is not ideological. *Power is an end in itself.* Anything that exists as an end in itself is God, practically speaking. God is the one entity that is not secondary or instrumental. Power, therefore, functions as God.

When Power becomes the primary and self-constituting thing, when Power becomes independent of and actually neutral in relation to principles or value – independent of ideology, in other words – then Power becomes the Thing That is God. You can see why people who have Power find it impossible to walk away from it willingly. It is the drug of life, not *a* drug.

If offered a third term to be President of the United States after having already served two, would you turn it down? Has anybody ever?

Mighty Mouse

Of all the religions that are not called religions, power is the mightiest of them all. Ideology, which provides to its partisans a license to kill and to dismiss, begins to fade when you start to suffer. A feminist theologian was dying from cancer a few years ago, and was visited in the hospital by another feminist theologian, a person I know well. The visitor was quite surprised when her old comrade-in-arms looked up at her and said, "What can feminist theology do for me now?"

Sex fades, at least for many men, but only at the point when the equipment is invaded by cancer or part of the brain shut down by cancer. I am amazed at how many 90-year-old men still have sex on their minds. Socrates was wrong about that.

Power, however, persists until the very moment consciousness ends. Have you ever been part of a "death watch" that had more to do with money than with the "loved one"? People really do change their wills during their last day on earth. Have you ever been with a rich old lady who rules the roost from her bed? Many times I have watched dying people divide and conquer, actively intimidating their adult children, who are easily intimidated, as it turns out.

Sedation of the dying has lessened this human phenomenon, which permeates the novels of Trollope and Eliot. But the impulse is there. "Hang on to your ego" (Beach Boys) until the final second.

The last act, holding on to your physical life, is an act of Power. If you don't have your physical life, then, and only then, do you not have Power. As a religion that is not called a religion, Power disappears, literally turns into smoke, only at the moment you separate from your body. Then, to use the phrase from English pubs, "It's time!"

Ranking religions that are not called religions

If this were an issue of *U.S. News and World Report*, a ranking would follow of the six religions that are not called religions; or, if you like, those sought-after things that are not called religions but act like religions. Like a college ranking, it could help you choose yours.

A ranking does follow. Number one, and they are in descending order, will go to the religion that has the longest life-expectancy. Note that none of these religions has anything to offer you after your death. These are all religions you can adopt during your life. This ranking can help you choose that informal religion which has the longest shelf-life in the world we actually know.

Here is the ranking:

ONE: Power. It has the longest shelf-life, and can be held from birth to death.

Two: Sex. It can be enjoyed from birth to almost death.

THREE: Ideology. It can be used to categorize and divide until you can't think any more.

Four: Family and children. Attending love is nice at the end, but at the very end it can only be received from one person. This person is rarely your child.

FIVE: Fame. People always like to be appreciated, but the older you get, the more you forget how famous you once were. "I used to be 'James Polk'."

Six: Things. These get old the moment you get them. They have the shortest shelf-life.

But Is There Anything to It?

Does God Exist?

"I once talked to the late Soviet physicist Lev Landau on this subject. The setting was a shingle beach in the Crimea.

'What do you think,' I asked, 'does God exist or not?'

There followed a pause of some three minutes.

Then he looked at me helplessly.

'I think so.'"[21]

The Onion: Is there a God?

Nick Lowe: [Long pause.] Yes.[22]

Can we talk about God for a minute? Not 'God' in quotes –

---

21 Andrei Tarkovsky, *Sculpting in Time*. Translated from the Russian by Kitty Hunter-Blair (New York: Alfred A. Knopf, 1987), 229.

22 As quoted by Stephen Thompson in "Is There a God?", *A.V. Club*, October 9, 2002.

the idea of God – but God. *Is there a God?* Is there anything objective to religion beyond the solely subjective? Did I find anything out about God – not 'God' – as a result of the collapse that took place in me on a Friday morning in January 2007?

Well, no, not really. Not then. Not yet.

BUT WAIT!: I haven't told you about 4.2.

I have to tell you about 4.2.

Race me to the bar!

I believe in God. I even believe God exists.

It's all the result of something that happened to me.

It was something so overwhelming that it erased all doubt in my mind.

And it had nothing to do with my lifetime of study.

I want to tell you about it now. I'll race you to the bar.

Here is what happened:

My wife Mary and I were visiting Chapel Hill, North Carolina, where we had both been undergraduates during the late 1960s. Neither of us had been back to Chapel Hill since the Spring of 1970.

I had left my 'Tar Heel' life in complete discomfiture.

It had to do with a girl and the end of an affair (Graham Greene).

It was the Spring of Kent State and the whole place, like every other American college campus, was in ferment.

Although the ferment was all around, it meant nothing to me personally.

All I could think about was how miserable I was.

Sure they were "singing songs and carrying signs" (Buffalo Springfield), but all I could think about was *her* and how bereft I felt.

Late one night I was returning a ton of books to the library "night deposit" chute. I was completely alone, returning a ton of books, as I say, to the library "night deposit" chute. This felt like a last official act before heading up north to a new school.

Over a radio somewhere in the darkness, I could hear The 5th Dimension singing "Age of Aquarius/Let the Sunshine In". I have never been so unhappy in my life.

The fact is, the next morning, during the 10-minute break between classes, I ran into a very pretty Brown Eyed Girl who would one day be my wife. We literally walked into each other! It was raining and all the co-eds had red or black parasols. *Umbrellas of Cherbourg.*

The Contraption (not The Antagonist)

Now it is 43 years later. It is 4.2.13: Monday the second of April in the year 2013. Miss Umbrellas of Cherbourg 1970 and I are walking down the same brick pathway where we had more or less collided the day after "The Age of Aquarius". The whole world has happened since that momentous day. And that day was the day after... the worst night of my life.

Suddenly, and this really happened, I saw something in the sky.

It was huge. It looked just like the floating space-galleon in *Time Bandits* (1981). It was a giant floating ship, that is what it looked like. It was creaking and kind of wafting and was completely complex, like the black-light UFO which floats over Richard Dreyfus in *Close Encounters of the Third Kind* in that scene when he stops his power truck by the mailboxes.

I knew immediately to call it the Contraption.

The Contraption was over our heads, drifting very gently. All I could hear was a kind of winding sound, or unwinding.

It was so physically powerful, seeing the Contraption over my head, that I felt I was being pushed backwards. Or was it forward? The feeling I had was a feeling of Total Awe.

"… shapes our ends"

What was it? What did I see?

It was a mystical experience, for certain, as real to me as typing this page is now. Mary didn't see the Contraption, although she knew something was happening with me. It was around two o'clock on a sunny afternoon, yet to me the sky had turned completely dark, like that night 43 years before.

The Contraption was in black light. And there it was, creaking its way across the sky, like a thousand pieces of interlocking wood.

What I knew there and then, on Monday April 2, 2013, is that God exists.

A night and day almost exactly 43 years earlier was bound to my April Morning *that* morning with a unity that could only "Take my Breath Away" (Berlin). It convinced me in five seconds, not ten minutes anymore, that God exists and I am in His mind. Mary, too. Hence everyone to whom we have given birth, and everyone to whom they have given birth, and everyone I have ever known.

So I wanted to race you to the bar, and tell you, as simply as possible, what it was that convinced me there is a God.

I don't expect you to agree with me. I do expect you to say, "OK, Paul, something happened to you. You say you saw the Contraption. It put everything together. I believe you."

Commemorative Plaque

Wish I could go back and put one up.

I would put it up right where it happened on 4.2.13, on the wall of the Carolina Playmakers Theater on the Old Campus of the University of North Carolina at Chapel Hill. I'd have them write, underneath the little explanation of what happened to me there, the following words:

ERECTED BY THE FRIENDS OF PAUL ZAHL

IN GRATEFUL APPRECIATION FOR THE ANSWER THAT FINALLY CAME.

Is There Life After Death?

Interestingly enough, I can take a stab at this one, too.

It was another thing that happened, as it turns out, though this time I want to theorize a little.

We are not doing our job, it seems to me, in relation to the lead character of this book, the man who's been "Bouncing off the Satellites" (B-52s) the whole time, if we don't try to help him with where he is going.

The lack of something to say, or is it a fear of saying something "pat" or facile, is a problem when you are trying to comfort the terminal.

For the entire 40 years I spent in the science of pastoral care, you were not supposed to talk about "the one thing needful" (Luke 10:42).

You weren't supposed to talk about Heaven.

If you spoke about Heaven, you were somehow not being "real" and dealing with the dying person as she or he supposedly was. Speaking about life after death was considered non-empathic. (Can you believe it?)

The American Protestant community, of which I was a long-standing member, had lost its nerve in connection with *that*. So you had better stick to *touch*, to being *with*, and to helping the dying *let go*. And I agreed with that so far as it went.

But it didn't go nearly far enough.

Going My Way (1944)

What I didn't agree with about it was its forced reticence concerning the one question everybody is asking: What is going to happen to me after I die?

A dying man or dying woman does best when they are able to let go because they are going some*where*. The fear you see in the faces of the dying – and I discern fear there much more often than acquiescence – is because they do not know where they are going. It's a pervasive fear. I have been with committed Christians who were certain of "where I'm going" their whole lives, but their certainty was shaken when they found out they were actually dying.

Being human, not-knowing translates into dread. Wherever or whatever it is that I am facing after my body and spirit detach from each other, it is probably bad.

So please, can you tell me something good? Can you tell me a little about where I am going?

Maria

On February 12, 1955, Maria Huxley, the first wife of Aldous Huxley, died. Aldous Huxley wrote a short account of her death. Here are three excerpts from it:

> "I continued to remind her of who she really was – a manifestation in time of eternal (*sic*), a part forever unseparated from the whole of the divine reality; I went on urging her to go forward into the light…

> "Let her forget the past, leave her old memories behind. Regrets, nostalgias, remorses, apprehensions – all these were barriers between her and the light. Let her forget them…

> "'Peace now.' I kept repeating. 'Peace, love, joy *now*. Being *now*.'… When the breathing ceased, at about six, it was without any struggle."[23]

---

23 As quoted by Laura Archera Huxley, *This Timeless Moment. A Personal View of Aldous Huxley* (New York: Farrar, Straus & Giroux, 1968), 24-25.

These words to a beloved wife from her loving husband express a great hope. They communicate a great innocence, which begins at death, and also a great union with the inseparability of God. They communicate the two learnings that lie behind this book: God makes us innocent for all that we have ever done, and there is no separateness between the inward reality of us and the invisible Reality of God. Add only my personal P.S., and I think we're set:

God is the Contraption, and He never stopped looking after us while we were here, even when we thought He had.

Something like this is what we need to be able to tell our "off the wall" friend, who is still in a holding pattern but for only a short time to go. What I have been holding back so far in this book is the fact that OUR FLOATER IS ABOUT TO DISAPPEAR. He is going to fade completely from sight the moment the doctors pronounce him dead. At that point we are truly going to lose him. His position has now become urgent.

Lakshmi

Aldous Huxley's last novel was called *Island*. It was published in 1962. In it he put into fictional form the farewell he had spoken to his wife Maria seven years earlier.

Huxley describes his character 'Lakshmi' as she is dying. Lakshmi is just like our "man on the moon", although *her* near death has put her over in the corner, where she watches her dying self from a distance of eight feet. Thankfully, her daughter-in-law 'Susila' is at the side of her bed, speaking of the clear light towards which the sick woman is actually moving all the time.

Laura

On November 22, 1963, the same day that John F. Kennedy was assassinated and that C.S. Lewis died, Aldous Huxley died. Laura, Huxley's second wife, said the same thing to her husband that Susila said to Lakshmi in *Island*, which is the same thing her husband had said to Maria in 1955[24]:

> "'Easy, easy, and you are doing this willingly and consciously and beautifully – going forward and up, light and free, forward and up toward the light, into the light, into complete love.'"

This is what needs to be said to a dying person. Dying is not *all* about the now. It is not all about empathy and physical touching. Dying is also about the future. We are going towards something, something of which an individual is just a fractional part. There is a merging to it that is incredibly warm.

And I'm not just talking out of my hat.

Grease on Daniels Road

Wouldn't you know, because "when it rains, it pours", that exactly one month after I saw the Contraption on April 2, 2013, something else happened. Wouldn't you know that "one thing leads to another" (INXS). As a result, I agree with what Aldous Huxley told Maria in 1955, and what 'Susila' told 'Lakshmi' in *Island*, and what Laura Huxley told her husband on November 22, 1963.

I agree with them all.

This is what happened.

---

24 *Ibid.*, 307.

I was driving home on the 1st of May from STAPLES at our local mall. There I had picked up an orange Sharpie and a composition book that was on sale for $1.04. I have the receipt. There was a light rain.

Just before I came to the bridge that goes over the freeway, I went straight through the front windshield and up into the sky. I was flying at a 50-degree angle.

Half a minute later I came back. Instantly the words came to me: "Your soul just left your body and went to where it will go when you die. You went right to it, and you will definitely live forever. But not as this man driving in the rain with his little items from STAPLES. Only the part of you who is really you went through the windshield."

I have to say that a scene from *Grease*, the movie (1978), also came to mind.

You remember it, where John Travolta and Olivia Newton-John ascend into heaven driving a big black Ford. That's what I did on Daniels Road on May 1, 2013. The dying me stayed in the car; the live-forever-me flew right through the windshield.

Formal and material

Now we are in territory where it's difficult to speak about things with much precision. Do you remember the distinction from philosophy class between "formal" and "material"? "Formal" refers to the outward shape, or form, of a thing – how it looks from the outside. "Material" refers to the content or substance of the thing – how it is on the inside.

When I went through the windshield on May 1, 2013, I was re-uniting with the formal or outward aspect of life. Life is one, being is one, all is one, "We Two Are One" (Eurythmics). I knew I was "going" to the one, that I had always been part of the one; and that even if I went back to my car and "Through the Looking Glass" again, like Alice, I would meet the one there. The formal property of me, the real and lasting me, was oneness.

Words are a problem when you try to talk about this. No wonder Gerald Heard never used the word 'God' if he could help it. Instead, he would always talk about "this thing".

But the oneness of which I felt sure was not the whole story. Flying through the windshield and up into the sky on Daniels Road the 1st of May was not the whole story. For I had also seen the Contraption! I had seen the Contraption a month before, on April 2nd. Seeing the Contraption had let me know that the one that was over me was also materially good and had never forgotten me. God was *one, formally*; but the one was *good, materially*.

Formal ether and material ether

Formal Ether is my phrase for Heaven. It is the oneness of being to which we are going and from which we came. It is undifferentiated. It means that I can communicate with you because underneath the "identity" that each of us carries, and which usually divides us, I am the same as you. This is why I can talk to you. It is also why I can love you. In the words of an old revivalist hymn, there is "Nothing Between".

But my other phrase for Heaven is Material Ether. The chief property of the being that is reality is love. The Contraption I glimpsed over Chapel Hill told me that God had never lost count of a single one of my days, nor a single one of my sorrows. I had never been forgotten. He was as good as He is real.

So I want to give a little speech to our friend, who's been off the wall, stuck on the ceiling, this whole time. I want to give a little speech. Hopefully, if he can hear it, and if the doctors haven't quite given up on him yet, there is still time. My speech is going to sound a little like Rod McKuen. But I like Rod McKuen.

Viaticum

"You are on your way, dear friend.
What you just left is behind you now. You can leave it there.
(God will take care of it all, together with the people you
    loved so much.
There was one especially.)
You are going to where you will always be understood.
Nothing you ever did and nothing you ever suffered was
    not understood.
Every trip and every kiss was part of the plan.
You are going to fly through the windshield that separates
    you from God.
You are going straight there, in the blink of an eye.
Listen:
Perfect love casts out fear."

I gave this speech I wrote to our friend because I believe what it says. I believe what it says because "mine eyes have seen".

Nunc dimittis.

198

Summary and Conclusion

"Let us, therefore, stop, while to stop is in our power:
let us live as men who are sometime to grow old."
-Samuel Johnson[25]

A person doesn't have to wait to the very last possible minute, like the subject to whom I have just given that little valedictory. It is still possible to make a change before then, before you are about to disappear. Dr. Johnson, in the above quotation from *Rasselas*, was trying to get through to the non-nearly dead. Likewise I am trying to get your attention *before* your stroke or your blockage or your pancreatic cancer. At least before you find yourself up there on the ceiling, like our friend, or in the corner of your room, like Lakshmi in *Island*.

Failed possibilities

By the time a person begins to realize he is dying, he has usually exhausted the possibilities he grew up hearing about, which purport to confront the human dilemma. By

---

25   Samuel Johnson, *Rasselas* in *A Johnson Reader*, Edited by E.L. McAdam, Jr. & George Milne (New York: The Modern Library, 1966), 252.

these I mean the organized religions of his childhood. He probably thinks he is more or less on his own now. "'There must be some way out of here', said the joker to the thief/ 'There's too much confusion, I can't get no relief'" (Bob Dylan). And there isn't.

Moreover, the possibilities for an exit that were promised by the religions that are not called religions, have failed him, too. His aging body has turned the promise of sex into a fixed and beautiful memory. The world has stopped *looking* at him – "Don't pass me by" (Ringo) – and he really is, now, starting to be forgotten. His hoarding of things has begun to overwhelm his space, like 'Charles Foster Kane'. He no longer has the physical strength to take old 'Rosebud' up to the attic. He has become the Queen of Versailles.

Moreover, the children are grown; and, as his wife has begun saying to him, "They have their own lives now." They don't like him very much, to tell you the truth.

Nor can ideology do much for him anymore. He has lived through so many cycles of hope for social improvement that he has become permanently disillusioned. Old ideologues are rare.

We have already talked about power. It is still in active currency, though it is quite cold.

No country for old men

From the standpoint of my own profession, I meet few old men who still practice their religion. Even if they were once active in the church, their heart is not in it any more. If his wife is alive and a churchgoer, an old man may accompany her to church – maybe he can usher at the 8 o'clock. But it has the feel of being habitual rather than heartfelt. For most old men I have known in the church, the "shades of the prison house" (Wordsworth) closed in long ago.

Even power, the last of the untitled religions to "go", gets to the point when it can hardly be used. The desire to have power, and hold on to it, is inherent. There are several people who have had it and are holding on to it now. They won't let go. Those people are terrible. Even Mr. and Mrs. Ceaușescu finally lost their power. They were shot, and their glassy eyes stared up to nothing in the muddy snow on which their bodies lay. The Ceaușescus were shot in haste. Did they have any idea that the end was really here?

Yet now I will bear witness:

There is still hope for the dying and near-dead.

'César Soubeyran'

We have a star witness.

It is 'César Soubeyran', the main character in *Manon of the Spring*. *Manon of the Spring* is a 1986 film by Claude Berri that is based on a novel by Marcel Pagnol. It is a story of hope being snatched from the jaws of total defeat in the life of its elderly protagonist. The resolution of *Manon of the Spring* turns upside-down, in one astonishing lightning strike, the cumulative disillusionment, suffering, and defeat of a life grown old.

'César Soubeyran', played by Yves Montand in this tale of crime, discovery, downfall, and retribution, has led a self-centered and self-deceived life. But events go in such a way that he is unexpectedly allowed to see the scale of the wrong he has done, and understand the fatal damage his actions have done to others whom he loved, and whom he should have loved. When César's eyes are suddenly and shockingly opened, *in very late old age*; when César is forced to see the cause and effects of a resentful, malicious life rooted in an ancient misunderstanding that took place in his youth, César collapses emotionally. The old man completely implodes. "Out, out, brief candle! Life's but a walking shadow" (*Macbeth*).

But wait! You have to wait:

César Soubeyran gets the rare chance to absorb what he has found out. He has seen what should never be seen, and rarely is. He sees the truth of his false and grasping self. But he does not enter hell as a result of it. Something else happens.

César breaks the ancient law of a pre-determined fate. He stops being a character out of Greek tragedy, the anvil of "The Force of Destiny" (Verdi), and makes urgent confession to a priest. The priest himself is a small-minded person, who can barely take in what is being told him. But César perseveres, and makes his full confession. He also makes, through a letter to someone and instructions to a lawyer, full restitution for the crime he committed.

César Soubeyran dies at peace. The last image of *Manon of the Spring* is the quintessence of what this book is about.

Double Vision

What does the lens of near-death experience see? What insights do impending dissolution give us, especially concerning religion? What has this guide to world religion finally decided ?

It has decided two things, but only two:

ONE, the only religion that will work for the dying is a religion of mercy. Total mercy is the only thing that will work. No evaluations, no comparisons, no critical assessments. And also, from our end, as with César Soubeyran at the end of *Manon of the Spring*, no defending and no rationalizing.

Two, we have to die invisibly to 'Paul Zahl', and 'César Soubeyran', and anyone else you want to name. We have to die to "baby driver". Baby driver guided us to hell. We wouldn't be in this "fine mess" if it hadn't been for baby driver. He was a willful blind guide. He was set on doing what he wanted to do. We should have noticed that he couldn't see.

People need to distance themselves from baby driver. Why should you wait until you are floating in the air, to fire the lead in this fatal drama, your own *Glass Menagerie*?

A great Amnesia from God

I am 62 years old. I have had a long career, a beautiful and inspiring wife, three great sons, and terrific grand-children. Yet the first of these things got crushed beyond recognition in my 56th year; and with it, the life-long baby driver who had answered to my name.

Like the sitcom characters who were looking for enlightenment, I started reading everything in sight. Then I started watching everything in sight.

Note to myself: I think I found what I was looking for.

What is it again?:

A different me, and a great Amnesia from God.

THE END

Appendix 1
Is Religion for the Young?

The wisdom of religion consists, according to this book, of two things:

Focussing on compassion and dis-attaching from the self that seems in charge but isn't. Grace and transcendence are two words for this wisdom, and that's about all there is.

But a question arises in the transmission of the wisdom.

It is not a *Curse of the Fly* problem, but it is an issue of transmission.

If the best way to understand truth is through the lens of one's death, what about the young? They are not programmed to think this way. It is not built in to them. Younger humans do not have the synapses, or whatever it is, that makes death a real subject.

How many funerals have I attended, and conducted, of teenagers killed in cars or because of overdoses. I found that the public displays of grief on the part of the dead teenager's friends were overwhelmingly embarrassing to me. They also seemed predictable, as if a switch had been flipped that read, "This is what you do when your high school friend is killed." There was extreme display but no *contact* I could see with the tragedy, or with the real feeling of the tragedy, the loss that had taken place. The p.d.a.'s (i.e., public displays of affection) came like a monsoon but they also left in about a day.

A teenaged parishioner of mine was killed by his best friend when they were playing with guns in the other boy's bedroom. I knew the boy well, and his family, too. It was absolutely the worst! Yet the huggings and weepings during the week that followed lacked endurance. I got to see the follow-up – up close. Yes, I thought the parents would probably never recover. But the friends, the girls and boys in the youth group and at school: it was the worst thing that had ever happened, and it was forgotten in a week.

What I am saying is that young people were not designed by nature to take in the wisdom that life is mostly futile, love is rarely lasting, and old age and dying make life seem unreal and almost like a joke. You can't say this to a young person. They not only don't like it, but it is unreal to them.

In *Rasselas*, Samuel Johnson's short novel published in 1759, a philosopher named Imlac accompanies a young prince and a young princess, together with her "favourite", i.e., the young girl friend of the princess, to visit an old man. The man is intelligent, and he is mindful and articulate concerning his declining body and his declining spirits.

As the three young people leave the old man, they reveal to Imlac their discomfort with the disillusionment to which the old man has just given voice. They begin to blame the old man for his discontents, and rationalize to themselves that the old man must be an exception.

Here is what Imlac thinks to himself after he listens attentively to the reactions of his young wards:

> "Imlac, who had no desire to see them depressed ... remembered that at the same age, he was equally confident of unmingled prosperity and equally fertile of consolatory expedients. He forbore to force upon them unwelcome knowledge, which time itself would too soon impress."[26]

Imlac "forbears" to "force upon them unwelcome knowledge".

He realizes that they cannot and will not hear the lessons about reality that the old man tried to teach. The old man was right, but the time was not right for the young inquirers who went to hear him.

Religious teachers often forebear in this way, like Imlac.

They see the human life cycle as impervious, until about age 40, or even 50, to the thought of one's personal death. So they don't teach it. They teach about limitations maybe, and wise "choices of life" – the phrase is Johnson's, as the young heroes of the story are determined to make the right "choice of life" – and to not over-extend themselves. Don't be fooled by "Bright Lights, Big City" (Jimmy Reed): the religions that are not called religions, such as sex, things,

---

26   Samuel Johnson, *Rasselas* in *A Johnson Reader,* Edited by E.L. McAdam, Jr. & George Milne (New York: The Modern Library, 1966), 302.

and fame. Religions that are not called religions are, as a young Buddhist teacher I met says to his young students, "unsatisfactory". Even the young should be able to see that.

Don't try to damage their aspirations, however. You only have one life to live, so goes the rationale, and they will find out soon enough that their ideas about life are a balloon that is easily pricked.

The practical consequence of this forbearance is that a wise teacher holds back part of what he or she has to say. The time is not right, so wait. I understand this. I was once addressing the weekly religious assembly of an independent school and forget to remember that my hearers were almost all under the age of 18. I let the cat out of the bag, and talked about careers as futile and self-concepts as fluctuating. They hated it! The poor chaplain had to do damage-control for a whole week. (Though after that it became as if my talk had never happened.)

The problem I have with keeping the wisdom of experience away from the young is that it means you are not being wholly truthful. You are not telling them what is actually going to happen. You are consciously trying not to rain on their parade, while anyone can see that a storm is brewing across the lake.

I understand why you would hold back on some truths for reasons of expedience. Who wants your youth group throwing stones at you and telling their parents they will never go back because of that depressing Paul Zahl?

I understand that.

I think I also grasp what wise teachers are saying when they say, "Even if you didn't hold back, and decided to tell them the incoming, oncoming truth, they wouldn't hear it anyway. People are made in such a way that the first half of their lives is immunized against those thoughts. It won't work, not for a minute, even if you do it."

The Buddha was questioned once about his having renounced the world at such a young age. Why, he was asked, did you not first live your youth in its vitality and force, and then *later* renounce and follow the way? Why didn't you take up religion in the second half of your life?

The Buddha answered that he had decided to renounce and go out on the road *because* he was young. As a young person, he knew he had the energy to really do it, and test it, and work it. He would have the time to learn the full meaning of a renounced life.

Think about St. Francis of Assisi and St. Ignatius Loyola in the Christian tradition. They started young. Yes, like the Buddha, they had suffered an early experience of contingency. Each had lost something big and had therefore seen. They started young because they saw when they were young.

In the Protestant tradition, Ulrich Zwingli, who became the Reformer of Zurich, is a classic instance of starting young. But why was he able to do so? Because he got the plague and almost died of it. That's why.

My issue with people who think the truth of life and dying should be held back in the case of young people, and even 30-year-olds, is that it is not the whole truth. Are you being truthful when you hold back, or consciously hold back, what you know?

Pedagogically speaking, holding back has a lot in its favor.

Philosophically and religiously speaking, I think it is questionable.

Have you ever wondered what would have happened if, when you were young, the self that you now are had been able to approach you and warn you? Many stories and plays have tried to visualize such a scene. Rod Serling staged this a couple of times in *The Twilight Zone*, and there is an episode of *Amazing Stories* in which the older version of a young woman on the verge of a disastrous mistake gets picked up on the side of the road. The older woman tries to convince her younger self not to do what she is about to do. The episode is called "Lane Change", and was broadcast in 1987.

I wonder about this myself. If only, I think to myself, a wiser and older person had warned me about thus and so. I realize now that a few people did try to warn me. Was I able to hear what they had to say? Not a chance.

So yes, you can't tell somebody something before they are ready to hear it.

Even so, should you withhold the truth, or an important part of it, in order to accommodate your student?

Let Samuel Johnson have the last word on this.

Is religion for the young?:

At the conclusion of *Rasselas*, in which the three young people, accompanied by Imlac, have explored the world in search of their "choice of life", they are gently led by him to a discussion concerning the soul.

After all their looking and peering and wandering, all their picaresque accidents and incidents, they are now open to "a new topick".[27] Johnson gives to the young princess the last word:

> "To me," said the princess, "the choice of life is become less important; I hope hereafter to think only on the choice of eternity."[28]

Religion, or rather the wisdom to be found in religion, is for the young.

But it seems they have to hit the wall first.

---

27 *Ibid.*, 307.

28 *Ibid.*, 313.

Appendix II
Should a Dying Christian Be Catholic, Protestant or Orthodox?

There are three main streams within Christianity and we owe it to the dying to say something about them. Or rather, we owe it to the dying to make a recommendation: If you are a Christian in name only, and most people in Western countries still are Christians even if in name only, then which one of the three possibilities could offer you the most when you are dying? After all, that is the one time when you may really be thinking about it. There is probably still wisdom in the old saying, "There are no atheists in foxholes."

In a thriller called *Seconds*, which came out in 1966 and starred Rock Hudson, there was a memorable moment when a man facing imminent death had to choose what kind of Christian he wanted to die as: Protestant or Catholic. He was also offered a Jewish option. He was extremely disturbed by the question, which is an understatement, in that he had never given it a moment's thought until that moment. We understood already that he was probably a nominal Episcopalian.

If you are a cultural Christian, and even many who answer, when they are polled about their religion, that they have "none", turn out to have been slightly raised in the church, or raised by parents who would have considered themselves to be Christians; and if you are having to prepare for death, then which of the formal Christian options has anything to say to you now?

It may sound hypothetical, but it's really not.

Under the condition of Dr. Johnson's "wonderful concentration of the mind" that a death sentence brings about, what *brand* of Christianity could help someone who "hasn't really thought about it before"? Let's pick up the panopticon again and see what we can see.

Catholic

In my opinion, a dying Christian does well to be an "R.C."

Catholicism changes less than Protestantism – it changes very little by most standards – and it's almost always in English now. You can count on Catholicism, because the priest, no matter who he is, can be counted on to do the properly predictable thing when he communicates you at the end. He will give you a real *viaticum*, bread and wine, or at least bread; and it will be the real sacrament, something you can see, taste and feel. He will also look like a priest, probably be nice like a priest – though "nice" is not guaranteed – and you will truly be on a list somewhere as a result. They won't forget you.

What is more, you can confess to him everything, like 'César Soubeyran' in *Manon of the Spring*. Time is short, but you can do it. The whole experience, if you are dying, will be concrete and embodied.

As a Protestant minister myself, I can recommend that you be a Catholic when it comes time for you to die.

Protestant

On this front, we can almost guarantee "nice". If the minister who is with you on your great Day – not forgetting the Aztec youths – is an evangelical Protestant, he will hopefully read to you from the Bible. The translation will be terrible, however. If you are "nominal", which I am saying you are, then you won't recognize a word of what he reads. Protestants, whether they are evangelical or liberal, change the translation they use of the Bible about every nine years.

Some ministers may badger you a little, but most actually won't. They just won't be predictable, or safely comforting. As a Protestant, there is no telling what you are going to get.

Charles Laughton, the famous actor who was very lapsed, asked for a priest to come to his bedside as he lay dying. Laughton was in fact a lapsed Catholic. He reported after the visit that he was glad the priest came. But he also said that he wished he'd gotten a better one!

My advice to you is that when it comes your time to be extremely sick, and you wish to speak with someone about religion, consider becoming a Catholic so it can be simple and reliable.

217

Orthodox

A huge advantage of being raised Orthodox is the way they marry people in church. Getting married according to the liturgy of Eastern Orthodoxy is truly wonderful! (Did you see *My Big Fat Greek Wedding* (2002)? Or did you read *Anna Karenina*?) The solemnity and symbolism of weddings in Orthodoxy suits absolutely the gravity of the occasion, an appropriate gravity which is often missed out on today by couples getting married.

As a minister, I have had it with "destination weddings". I hate standing on beaches at 6 pm, no matter where it is: the sun is almost always directly in your face if you are the officiant. You have to wear sunglasses, and it makes you think you're in a scene in *Miami Vice*.

Give me St. George's Orthodox Church any time! Believe it or not, I think most couples feel the same way afterwards.

Orthodoxy in English-speaking countries has a chronic problem, though: the service is usually in Greek. Also, you have to stand for a lot of it. Americans find this hard; and newcomers, who often really *want* the lofty verticality of this beautiful religion, are severely tested by the Greek and by the lengthy standing.

I still think being Catholic is probably best for a dying cultural Christian.

But when you're actually dead:

Then you should be Episcopalian!

There is nothing comparable in the whole galaxy of Christian churches to the burial service of *The Book of Common*

Prayer. It is lofty, like the Orthodox Church, but in English; serene; non-preachy; and it combines a spirit of quiet thanksgiving for the dead with hope in the resurrection of the dead.

When you are actually dead, be an Episcopalian.

There is one small but not insuperable problem. Call it a problem in the transmission, as we have encountered them before: the Episcopalians rarely use their greatest asset. They changed the service in 1979, and made it more "upbeat" in tone and therefore less sublime, and less profound. So make sure you request – but you won't be there so it will have to be a member of your family – the service known as "Rite One". It begins on page 469.

Recommended Reading

Henri Bergson, *The Two Sources of Morality and Religion*, translated by R. Ashley Audra and Cloudesley Brereton with the assistance of W. Horsfall Carter (Garden City, N.Y.: Doubleday & Company, Inc., 1935).

Algernon Blackwood, *Incredible Adventures* (London: MacMillan and Co., Limited, 1914).

Emil Brunner, *The Misunderstanding of the Church*, translated by Harold Knight (Philadelphia: The Westminster Press, 1953).

Robert Farrar Capon, "Preface" to his *The Romance of the Word* (Grand Rapids, MI: William B. Eerdman's Publishing Company, 1995).

The Compassionate Buddha, edited with commentary, by E.A. Burtt (New York: The New American Library, 1955).

Harvey Cox, *Turning East: The Promise and Peril of the New Orientalism* (New York: Simon and Schuster, 1977).

David Flusser, *Jesus* (Jerusalem: Magnes Press, Hebrew University of Jerusalem, 1997).

James Gould Cozzens, *By Love Possessed* (New York: Harcourt, Brace and Company, 1957).

James Gould Cozzens, *Men and Brethren* (Chicago: Elephant Paperbacks, 1989).

John Galsworthy, *Flowering Wilderness* (New York: Charles Scribner's Sons, 1932).

John Galsworthy, *One More River* (New York: Charles Scribner's Sons, 1933).

Great Tales of Terror and the Supernatural, edited by Herbert A. Wise & Phyllis Fraser (New York: The Modern Library, 1944).

Aldous Huxley, *Eyeless in Gaza* (London: Chatto & Windus, 1936).

William Inge, *Good Luck, Miss Wyckoff* (Boston and Toronto: Little, Brown and Company, 1970).

William Inge, *My Son is a Splendid Driver* (Boston and Toronto: Little, Brown and Company, 1971).

Christopher Isherwood, *Diaries Volume One: 1939-1960*, Edited and introduced by Katherine Bucknell (London: Vintage, 1997).

Christopher Isherwood, "The Day at La Verne", *The Penguin New Writing*, July-September 1942, 12-14 (Harmondsworth: Allen Lane Penguin Books, 1940-1950).

Vedanta for the Western World, Edited and with an Introduction by Christopher Isherwood (Hollywood: Vedanta Press, 1945).

Samuel Johnson, *Rasselas* in *A Johnson Reader*, edited by E.L. McAdam, Jr. & George Milne (New York: The Modern Library, 1966).

Recommended Reading

Jack Kerouac, *Desolation Angels* (New York: Riverhead Books, 1995; originally published in 1965).

Martin Luther, *A Commentary on St. Paul's Epistle to the Galatians, Based on Lectures Delivered by Martin Luther at The University of Wittenberg in the Year 1531 and First Published in 1535*, translated by Erasmus Middleton, edited and introduced by Philip S. Watson (Cambridge, U.K.: James Clarke & Co., 1953).

Robert Nathan, *The Bishop's Wife and Two Other Novels* (New York: Alfred A. Knopf, Inc., 1938).

The New Oxford Book of Christian Verse, edited by Donald Davie (Oxford: Oxford University Press, 2003).

The Oxford History of the Classical World, edited by John Boardman, Jasper Griffin and Oswyn Murray (Oxford and New York: Oxford University Press, 1986).

John van Druten, *The Widening Circle: A Personal Search* (New York: Charles Scribner's Sons, 1957).

H.R. Wakefield, *Strayers from Sheol* (Sauk City, Wisconsin: Arkham House, 1961).

The Best Ghost Stories of H. Russell Wakefield, selected and introduced by Richard Dalby (Chicago:Academy Chicago, 1982).

Mika Waltari, *The Dark Angel*, translated by Naomi Walford (New York: G.P. Putnam's Sons, 1953).

Mika Waltari, *The Egyptian*, translated by Naomi Walford (New York: G.P. Putnam's Sons, 1949).

H.G. Wells, *Mind at the End of its Tether* (New York: Didier, Publishers, 1946).

Paul F.M. Zahl, *2000 Years of Amazing Grace* (Lanham, MD: Rowman & Littlefield Publishers, 2006).

Paul F. M. Zahl, *The First Christian* (Grand Rapids, Michigan/ Cambridge, U.K.: William B. Eerdmans Publishing Company, 2003).